Beyond
the
Fence

Mixteca grandmother, mother and son pose on their front steps next to their kitchen garden.

Beyond
the
Fence

A Journey to the Roots of the Migration Crisis

Dori Stone

FOOD FIRST BOOKS
Oakland, California

Food First Books
398 60th Street
Oakland, CA 94618
510-654-4400
www.foodfirst.org

Cover and text design: Amy Evans McClure
Cover and interior photographs: Leonor Hurtado and Dori Stone
Production: Martha Katigbak-Fernandez
Copy editor: Carrie Laing Pickett
Proofreaders: Marilyn Borchardt and Martha Katigbak-Fernandez

LIBRARY OF CONGRESS CATALOGING-IN-PUBLICATION DATA
 Stone, Dori, 1983–
 Beyond the fence : a journey to the roots of the migration crisis / Dori Stone.
     p. cm.
   Includes bibliographical references.
   ISBN 978-0-935028-33-1
   1. Migrant agricultural laborers—Mexican-American Border Region.
   2. Alien labor, Mexican—Mexican-American Border Region. 3. Agriculture—
   Mexico. 4. Mexican-American Border Region—Emigration and immigration.
   I. Institute for Food and Development Policy (Oakland, Calif.) II. Title.
 HD1525.S76 2009
   331.6'2720721—dc22   2009002464

Food First Books are distributed by:
Perseus Distribution
387 Park Avenue South
New York, NY 10016
www.perseusdistribution.com

5   4   3   2   1

Contents

Chapter 2 • Chihuahua

Chapter 3: Mexico City

Preface

All people, even indigenous peoples, have migration as part of their history. Understanding diasporas both present and past is essential for coming to grips with our history and our sense of place, and for envisioning a better future.

Dori Stone's journey from the hollowed-out border town of El Paso, south along the "immigrant trail" to the desolate mountains of Oaxaca, is a story of discoveries—some painful, others hopeful, all deeply insightful. Dori chronicles both the structural causes and the human dimensions of the current migration crisis, one of the most profound demographic transformations in the history of the Americas.

The heated political debates on U.S. immigration often drown out the wrenching realities of migration itself. This book's refreshing prose gives a powerful voice to the families struggling with those realities. With relentless honesty, Dori's inquisitive pen weaves through U.S. and Mexican landscapes blighted by decades of free trade agreements. Somehow, she always uncovers creativity, intelligence, solidarity, and compassion among the people who have been forced to endure but refuse to succumb to the political and economic forces uprooting and transforming their way of life. The net effect is both sobering and inspiring, inviting us to become a part of the many hopeful alternatives and solutions being forged by thousands of farmers, communities, and activists on either side of the Rio Grande.

In the face of what would seem an intractable crisis, Dori Stone has indeed taken us "beyond the fence."

Eric Holt-Giménez

Acknowledgments

My heartfelt gratitude to the sponsors who enabled me to participate in the *El Camino del Migrante* reality tour: Mark Van Horn, Damian Parr, Kristin Reynolds, Kori Farrell, Chuck Amador, Dan Chase, Kaleen Perlich, Quill Chase, Chaponica Trimmell, Jan and Ernie Perlich, John Warren, Jean Stafford, the Stone Family, Rainbow Vogt, Paul Marcotte, Keren Ram, Catherine Peacock, Louisa Bohne Cardinali, Paul and Susan Paolilli, Penny Leff, Katherine Baker, Susan Lara, Paula Motlo, George and Nancy Sackman, Bill Fairbanks, John Beccia, Sheila Wynn, Dwayne DeVries, Raoul Adamchak, Nancy Koren, Dena Paolilli, and Agrarian Effort Co-op. Without your generous support, this book would never have been written.

Thank you to the staff of Food First, especially Eric Holt-Giménez and Marilyn Borchardt, for giving me this opportunity and for all your help, patience, guidance, and support along the way.

I am tremendously grateful to Angus Wright, Eric Greening, Ilona Stone, Kelly Tan, and Phil Dahl-Bredine for taking time to review the original manuscript, tackle my myriad questions, and offer such insightful feedback and suggestions. I have learned a great deal from you.

Thank you also to Leonor Hurtado for your enthusiasm and beautiful photographs, to Maria Barrera for so many hours of diligent research, to Rachel Fields for inspiring the opening lines of this book, and to Miranda Thompson, Sibongile Lungu, Venus Rivera, and Marisol Lopez for each contributing in your own priceless ways.

Above all, deepest thanks to Keren Ram and to my parents, Barry and Ilona Stone, for your ongoing encouragement and love.

And finally, to the many activists, farmers, and community members we met at the border and in Mexico, thank you for welcoming us into your lives and openly sharing your stories and experiences. Thank you for your perseverance in the face of oppression, and for giving us all cause to hope and to keep moving forward.

Introduction

The immigration debate in the United States is highly controversial, emotional, and often confusing. Each year, as the U.S. government spends billions of dollars trying to keep people out, approximately five hundred thousand new undocumented migrants cross the border from Mexico and disperse throughout the United States, taking low-wage jobs in cleaning, construction, manufacturing, food preparation, and, most notably, agriculture, where they comprise over half the U.S. migrant and seasonal farm-labor force. Each year, several hundreds of these migrants perish from heat and dehydration in the Arizona desert, and in most cases their deaths go unreported, their bodies uncounted, their families simply never hearing from them again. Yet despite the well-known risk of the journey, hundreds of thousands more—working-age men and women, grandparents, even young children—continue to leave their homes and embark on the migrant trail. Behind them, in rural Mexico, remittance money trickles into half-deserted villages where only the very old and young remain, and the soil of abandoned cornfields erodes steadily away down the mountainsides. Ahead of them, at the border, thousands will be apprehended and deported by *la migra* (U.S. border patrol), only to turn around and make the journey again, and yet again, until they either succeed or die in the attempt. The number of these migrants has skyrocketed since the 1980s, causing some analysts to describe it as "the largest mass migration in U.S. history."[1]

Although the roots of this phenomenon are tangled and its impacts varied, discussion of Mexico–U.S. migration here at home has tended to focus narrowly on a few specific issues of national security, border enforcement, social services, guest-worker programs, and earned legalization. Meanwhile, little attention has been given to the underlying causes driving hundreds of thousands to leave their homes in the first place, and even less attention to the possible alternatives that might allow them to remain and prosper in their own communities.

In hopes of exploring these neglected aspects of the immigration dilemma, the Institute for Food and Development Policy/Food First organized a ten-day reality tour in the summer of 2007, allowing members of the public to travel to the border and deeper into Mexico, where we could witness firsthand the impacts of migration and learn about the largely unpublicized yet growing movement toward true, tangible solutions.

Having recently graduated with a bachelor of science degree in international agricultural development from the University of California, Davis, I was excited by the opportunity to participate in this trip. Aside from occasional newspaper articles, radio broadcasts, and brief conversations, I knew very little about Mexico–U.S. migration. I had no regular contact with migrant workers, and only a general awareness of the conditions causing these people to leave their homeland.

However, I had spent the past few years working in agriculture, reading and discussing topics of international development, and participating in grassroots organizations focusing on the pursuit of sustainability and social justice, so I felt sufficiently prepared to delve into this issue, ask lots of questions, and absorb all the details of what promised to be a very full and influential experience.

The following pages are based on observations and personal reflections I recorded in my notebook during that ten-day journey, along with background information that I researched upon returning home in order to provide the appropriate historical and political context for this account.

Although I learned a great deal during the trip and through subsequent research, I do not claim to be an expert on the topics presented here. I have simply written from the standpoint of a fellow citizen who took a trip and wants to relate what she saw and heard, so that others may partake in that journey as well. By sharing my observations and questions and ideas, I hope to raise new questions for you, the reader, and hope you will use this book as a launching pad for further reading, deeper understanding, and more effective dialogue, so that together we can begin to address these most pressing issues.

What you will find in the following pages are aspects of migration largely unnoticed by the public and mainstream media. These are the root causes and complex realities, the stories and surprising possibilities that get lost in a debate over fences. They are the tales of people's desperation and irretrievable loss, but also of their growing visions for hope. They were told to me by farmers and politicians and activists on both sides of the border, in village cornfields and city streets and conference rooms, and I now pass their stories along to you.

Food First Reality Tour Participants

Our trip was led by Food First executive director Eric Holt-Giménez, who has been directly involved with peasant movements and sustainable agriculture in Mexico and Central America for more than thirty years. For later reference, the other tour participants were:

Annette Hiatt • North Carolina lawyer working with the Land Loss Prevention Project, a nonprofit law firm that provides free representation for farmers and other low-income people struggling to keep their land

Brian Emerson • Graduate student of environmental studies at the University of California, Santa Cruz

Chia Hamilton • Resident of Oakland, California, and a third-generation activist working with People's Grocery, New Village Press, and Population Connection

Claudia Meléndez • Reporter for *The Monterey County Herald* in California, grew up in Mexico, and frequently writes about issues of immigration and the Latino community

Denise Ames • Community college teacher in Albuquerque, New Mexico, currently developing an agriculture and food systems curriculum

Jan Kindell • Community garden volunteer, board member of the Rio Grande Valley Farmers Guild, and facilitator for the growers of Sanchez Farm in Albuquerque, New Mexico

Laura Miller • Food First intern and recent graduate in international development studies at the University of California, Berkeley

Leonor Hurtado • Food First volunteer, environmental justice and human rights activist whose most recent work has been with indigenous communities affected by the mining industry in her home country of Guatemala

Marilyn Borchardt • Food First development director and intern coordinator for the past twenty-three years

Martha Robbins • International coordinator for the National Farmers' Union in Saskatchewan, Canada; received a yearlong fellowship to study issues relating to Mexican migrant farmworkers in Canada

Rachel Fields • Food First intern and student of community studies at the University of California, Santa Cruz

Sue Poyneer • Teacher of small business management at City College of San Francisco who is working on starting a certificate program in green and sustainable business

Trevor Mckenzie-Smith • Activist and political organizer for the New Democratic Party in Saskatchewan, Canada

We were also accompanied by award-winning filmmaker Juan Carlos Zaldívar, who has taught at the undergraduate film program at New York University and whose work has aired on PBS and at the Sundance Film Festival. Juan Carlos joined our trip and created a short documentary, *Caminos: The Immigrant's Trail*, which is now available through Food First.

Food First tour participants from the U.S. and Canada in a field at La Loma Ejido of Cuauhtemoc, Chihuahua.

Beyond the Fence

Borderlands

El Paso, Texas • July 30th, 2007

The Border Farmworkers' Center in El Paso, Texas, a homeless shelter and resource center for migrant farmworkers

We begin our trip at the U.S.-Mexico border, a busy corridor between countries, a region where thousands of migrants have come to labor in fields and factories on both sides of the fence. The city of El Paso is a major recruitment site for farmworkers, who arrive here before heading out to all other agricultural regions of the country, so it makes sense to me that our journey, with its goal of viewing migration through a direct, up-close lens, would begin here.

Our first stop of the day is *El Centro de los Trabajadores Agrícolas Fronterizos*, the Border Farmworkers' Center, where we catch a brief glimpse into the lives of migrant workers in this region. Up to 150 homeless laborers live in this building, working in the multimillion-dollar chile industry in southern New Mexico and returning at night for a hot meal and a place to spread their sleeping bags.

The center is a modern one-story building with big windows and a small grassy yard, located on a street corner in one of the oldest districts of El Paso. In plain view just a couple hundred yards away lies the border itself, a tall chain-link fence dividing the sprawl of El Paso from the even larger sprawl of Ciudad Juárez. We can see a steady flow of people walking north across one of the nearby pedestrian bridges, just a fraction of the thousands who live in Mexico and cross daily for their jobs in the U.S.

One of our guides for the day is Javier Perez, a young activist and college student in El Paso who helps run the farmworkers' center. We gather around Javier on the front lawn as he explains his work and answers questions. Intrigued by our surroundings, I scribble hastily in my notebook, not wanting to lose a single detail.

Just across the street from where we stand are several Homeland Security buildings with a lookout tower and high barbed wire fence. When the border patrol catches illegal crossers or undocumented workers, Javier says, that's where they hold them. It strikes me as an ironic neighbor for the farmworkers' center, but Javier explains that most of the residents here are actually documented, thanks to 1986 legislation that granted legal residency to nearly three million migrant workers.[1] Of course El Paso has its undocumented population as well, but they are mainly served by another local shelter.

On the sidewalk next to the building, a group of men hang out talking, accordion-laced *norteño* music streaming from a small boom box on the pavement. Others lie against the walls, wrapped in sleeping bags and flattened cardboard boxes, and Javier explains that they weren't allowed to sleep inside because they drank too much the night before. The farm workers who stay here make their own rules, he says, and they don't allow anyone who's drunk. When you're getting only four to six hours of sleep a night, you just want a quiet place to rest without troublemakers. But unfortunately, news reports tend to focus on these hungover people outside, not the ones who slept indoors and left for work hours ago.

Alcohol is a problem here, Javier admits, because even though the farms sometimes provide food and water, they nearly always sell beer, sometimes at a cheaper price than water. After harvesting chile peppers in the hot sun all day for low wages, that must look like a pretty good deal. And the buses coming back to El Paso in the evening stop at bars as well, so people arrive at the center with beers in hand and are forced to sleep outside.

Posted on the front windows of the building are info sheets about workers' compensation laws in Texas, two notices for missing women, an ad for a local health clinic, and a flier for employment opportunities in Alabama. You could leave the border and get hired as a truck loader, forklift operator, assembler, pallet builder, all sorts of things. . . .

These jobs are probably higher paying and more desirable than agricultural labor, I think to myself, *but they may also be harder to get, if you have no legal papers.*

Inside the entryway are more job notices: Four men needed at a dairy near Denver, Colorado, $1,500 per month, housing provided. Bacon-processing jobs in Ohio, $8.25 per hour, papers required, a recruiter will visit soon. Eric[2] reads over the sign and comments on the dangerous nature of meat-processing jobs, how people's arms and hands can get all sliced up.

Are these sorts of jobs so dangerous and physically demanding that only desperate migrants, without any better options, will take them, I wonder to myself, *or does the presence of a foreign-born and easily exploited workforce just pull the standards down, so that such conditions **can** be imposed? I suppose it's the old question of whether migrants are taking jobs away from U.S. citizens, who might leap to fill those spots if they had a chance. . . . Is that true? Would unemployed Americans take the meat-packing and truck-loading and pallet-building jobs, if they could? Perhaps it's a vicious cycle, in which migrants receive these jobs because they're willing to accept poor conditions and wages, which perpetuates those standards, which **makes** it "the work nobody else wants to do." What would happen, then, if federal labor standards were suddenly to rise, or were just more rigorously enforced? Would more U.S. citizens start competing for those jobs, and domestic employment rates increase? Would this country's demand for cheap imported labor begin to dry up? And if so, what would happen to the migrant workers so desperate for jobs as well?*

My mind starts to spin, and I follow everyone inside the farmworkers' center, hopeful that more answers will emerge later in our journey.

The main room of the center is a large open space with a colorful tile floor and faded photographs from the Bracero Program[3] lining the walls. There's also a small cafeteria with several tables and a Coca Cola machine, the daily menu, and a flier for free GED classes at El Paso Community College.

About sixty-five men and women are living here right now, Javier tells us, but when chile season picks up in a couple weeks, those numbers will more than double. The official capacity is only 120, but nobody is turned away. Sometimes more than 150 people stay here at a time, squeezing into every available spot in the offices and kitchen and cafeteria, just to lay down their sleeping bags and catch a few hours of sleep.

And it's really only a few: The workday for chile harvesters here begins around midnight, when labor contractors arrive in the streets of South El Paso to select and hire crews for the day. The buses leave at about 2 a.m. for their long drive out to the fields, where pickers work from dawn until mid-afternoon, wait another hour or two to get paid, and finally ride back to El Paso. They typically arrive at the center around 6 p.m., which leaves only a few hours to eat dinner, relax, and get some sleep before midnight rolls around again.

When you add all that time spent waiting, traveling, and working, it comes to at least sixteen hours per day, in exchange for about thirty dollars. (Chile pickers are paid per bucket harvested, but not all the workers can go fast enough—literally thousands of peppers per hour—to earn minimum wage.) I try to imagine how this would feel, leaving for work at midnight and arriving back home at 6 p.m. for only thirty bucks, day after day . . . and a troubling question keeps tugging at my mind: *Where do we draw the line between employment and slavery?*

With such low wages, it's little wonder that the workers are unable to afford housing. Even a cheap trailer or apartment is out of reach unless shared by a large group of people, and these homes commonly lack basic infrastructure such as running water and appliances. If you're working in the U.S. in order to support a family back home, is it really worth spending the majority of your income on such housing?

This is why the farmworkers' center is such a vital resource for the homeless laborers here in El Paso—many of them once slept on the streets and bridges in order to be at recruitment sites by midnight. After ten years of struggle, the farmworkers' center was finally built as a safe haven for those workers, a place where they can now sleep without danger of harassment and can receive a free meal and a place to shower. A local doctor gives free medical exams each week in the center's tiny clinic (particularly important since many of the workers suffer from skin problems related to pesticide exposure), and the center also offers regular English classes, workshops on labor rights and protecting oneself in the fields, assistance in filling out legal forms, and a space for the workers to gather and organize. Overall, it seems to function as a community center, a home base for the marginalized farmworker population of El Paso.

Back in March, for César Chávez Day, the center got lots of publicity, and people started calling to ask, "Is it true that you have no mattresses or cots for people? Why not?"

"No money," Javier explained. It took many years simply to get the funding to build this facility, and the farmworkers' center gets along as best it can. Even though he doesn't appreciate the accusatory tone of some questions, Javier is glad to see a growing concern from the public.

Except for a young woman at the front desk and those few people on the sidewalk, the place is empty at this hour of the morning, so we look around briefly and then head back to the vans, planning to return later in the day.

The Borderworker Center on the El Paso border with Mexico provides services for migrant farmworkers, including a spot to sleep on the floor.

Conditions for U.S. Farmworkers

In the 1960s, farm labor activist César Chávez began a nationwide move-ment that led to the creation of the country's first farm labor union (United Farm Workers of America) and new legislation to protect farmworkers under basic federal labor laws, from which they had originally been excluded. The Fair Labor Standards Act was amended in 1966 to include farmworkers under minimum wage laws, and, in 1987, a federal court forced the Occupational Safety and Health Administration (OSHA) to man-date basic sanitation standards such as toilets, hand-washing facilities, and potable drinking water in the fields. Yet despite these milestones, approxi-mately three million migrant and seasonal farmworkers in the U.S. today continue to face serious challenges and do not always receive the rights promised them by law. Cal/OSHA inspections in 1997 found over 50 per-cent noncompliance with the sanitation standards, and a U.S. Department of Labor survey from 2002 revealed that a significant portion of employers still failed to provide drinking water and sanitary facilities. Other common issues faced by farmworkers include:

- musculoskeletal damage, due to long hours of repetitive tasks in awk-ward positions
- lack of affordable health care
- heat stress, causing illness and occasional fatalities
- hundreds of pesticide poisoning cases per year, and lack of adequate pesticide-use training
- high rates of cancer among farmworkers and agricultural communities
- substandard housing (overcrowded, structurally unsound, lacking functional plumbing and appliances)
- a decline in real wages, with 60 percent of farmworker families now liv-ing below the official poverty level
- employment through labor contractors, who often exploit workers and pay lower wages

Some states have passed their own laws to protect farmworkers, but even in California, with higher labor standards and more collective bargaining in agriculture than any other state, less than 10 percent of farm-workers are covered by union contracts. The laws that exist are inade-quately enforced, and penalties for violations are low. This is compounded by the fact that over half of the current farmworkers are undocumented migrants, with even lower wages and less bargaining power than legal workers. Most migrants have risked their lives crossing the border to take farm jobs, and, due to their unauthorized status, extreme poverty, and lack of other opportunities (in the U.S. or at home), they are reluctant to complain about poor conditions.

The farm labor activism spearheaded by César Chávez in the 1960s is still alive today. The Coalition of Immokalee Workers, a farmworker organizing group in Florida, has successfully raised wages for tomato pickers for the first time in over twenty years, organized a major strike to protest beatings in the fields, and convinced state authorities to appropriate money for new housing in farmworker communities in Florida. Some U.S. employers are taking steps to improve labor conditions on their farms as well. Almost three hundred farms and ranches in the U.S., Canada, and Mexico belong to the Food Alliance, a nonprofit organization that certifies farms for providing fair labor conditions and wages, and the Agriculture Justice Project in the U.S. upper Midwest has recently begun a pilot project selling local, fair trade food products. Drafted after years of stakeholder input, the organization's new social stewardship standards include the right to collective bargaining, fair wages, workplace health and safety, and adequate housing. The slightly higher price of certified food allows these small-scale and family-owned farms to provide such benefits to their workers, for (unlike large corporate operations) many smaller producers are unable to afford health insurance for *themselves*, let alone their employees! According to David Lighthall of the California Institute for Rural Studies, the poor conditions endured by farmworkers are a "hidden cost" of food production, which will only be improved through a "broadening of responsibility to the larger public."

(See reference section for source material.)

Colonia *settlements along the U.S.-Mexico Border, and a conversation with children across the border fence*

Driving through neighborhoods of tidy little homes and apartments near the farmworkers' center, we learn that this whole area is subject to the city's "urban redevelopment plan," which includes new housing and commercial space—strip malls, parking garages, and a big-box retail store—right in the middle of El Paso's oldest neighborhood and long-established Mexican American community. The area consists almost entirely of Mexican immigrant families, who would be evicted and "resettled" in other neighborhoods, farther from the border and their family members living in Juárez. Apparently these residents and local businesses were never invited to the planning table, and the project is to be implemented by private out-of-state developers who stand to profit from the so-called revitalization of old El Paso.

Back on the border highway, we drive alongside the cement-lined canal of the Rio Grande, flanked on both sides by chain link and barbed wire fences, flood lights, occasional surveillance cameras mounted on poles, and dirt tracks where border patrol vehicles drive slowly back and forth. On the other side we can see Juárez, Mexico's fifth largest city, a matrix of streets and traffic and buildings stretching on into the desert, bordered by distant mountains of stark metamorphic rock. This entire metropolis feels surreal to me, strangely situated in such a vast, arid, inhospitable environment of barren rock and sky.

Rolling along the highway, we pass several large industrial plants on both sides of the fence, including the hundred-year-old ASARCO copper smelter that the state of Texas may soon reopen. During its operation, this plant released huge amounts of arsenic, lead, and other heavy metals into the air shared by nearby residential neighborhoods, contributing to the border region's high rate of respiratory disease and elevated levels of lead in children's blood. The smelter shut down in 1999 with over a hundred civil environmental cases pending against it, for everything from illegal disposal of hazardous waste to noncompliance with air quality standards. But now, ASARCO (a subsidiary of the multibillion dollar corporation Grupo México, one of the largest mining companies in the world) is seeking to renew its air quality permit and begin operating here again.[4]

We soon enter New Mexico and turn off the highway, following a short unpaved road to the border itself. Out here, it's just one long fence snaking through the desert, occasional holes patched up with wire, tire tracks in the dirt along the U.S. side. Two patrol trucks are parked nearby, the men inside watching us, probably wondering what strange sort of tourists would come *here*.

We climb out of the vans and stand at the border, taking everything in. The sky is sunny and clear today, but the valley below us lies under a haze of smog. Beyond some mounds of dirt and rubble on the other side of the fence are a group of ramshackle houses, which apparently lie at the edge of Colonia Anapra. I've heard of this sprawling border slum, an outgrowth of Ciudad Juárez that sprang up in the 1980s as migrants from southern Mexico began arriving to work in the *maquiladoras*.[5]

Mexican brother and sister speak with tour participants across the border near Sunland Park, New Mexico as border guards watch in the background on the U.S. side.

Although the government provided infrastructure (paved roads, power lines, running water, and so on) to the new factories, it did little to support this influx of workers. The result is Anapra, a haphazard development where thousands of families live in makeshift shelters of cardboard, cinderblock, corrugated tin and scraps of plywood, without running water or sewage systems. Only a few small structures are visible from where we stand, but it's striking to think how many stretch out beyond them.

Two children come walking over, a girl and a boy of grade school age. They stare at us shyly through the fence, and we try to strike up conversation. Their names are Jasmín and Arón, they tell us, and they live right over there, and it's vacation time from school. Their mom cleans houses and their dad works at a pizza place. They like to play here, among the little hills of sand and rubble.

Jasmín does the talking, standing at the fence and answering our questions in a soft, high voice.

"Have you ever been over to this side?" Juan Carlos asks.

"No," she replies.

"Do you want to come?"

"Yes."

"Yes? Why?"

She pauses and thinks about it for a moment. "I don't know."

When the questions stop, they just stand there watching us quietly. "Is it okay if we take your photo?" some people ask, and Jasmín smiles and nods. It's probably exciting to her, but I still feel awkward, standing on the American side of this fence and treating the kids like some sort of exhibit. Not to mention that the camera I'm using was made by Sony, a company with large maquiladoras along the Mexican border. For all I know, someone in her family helped *make* this thing, working in a factory all day and carrying traces of toxic residue back home on her skin and clothing. Trying to get past these discomforts and ironies, I point and click. Perhaps it can be justified, based on our motives, but I know it will never really feel okay.

"Are *la migra* always parked over there?" I ask.

The little boy nods, and I wonder what it's like to grow up next to a fence that's built especially to keep you out. I wonder if he'll cross it someday.

U.S.-Mexico border fence in New Mexico to be replaced by a steel plate fence as part of the planned 670 miles of reinforced fence.

The U.S.-Mexico Border Fence

Debate over the U.S.-Mexico border, particularly in the context of national security, has increased since September 2001. The Secure Fence Act of 2006 directed the Department of Homeland Security (DHS) to add 850 miles of new fencing and surveillance equipment along the two-thousand-mile border, a project the Congressional Budget Office has estimated at over three million dollars per mile.

Such a move is highly controversial, as indicated by a 2008 Ipsos-Public Affairs poll showing 49 percent of the American public in favor, 48 percent opposed, and 55 percent expressing little confidence that a fence would reduce illegal entries into the country. DHS Secretary Michael Chertoff claims that heightened security has *already* reduced crossings in fenced areas and possibly helped prevent terrorist attacks in the United States as well, yet the Immigration Policy Center of the American Immigration Law Foundation counters that no terrorists have been caught at the U.S.-Mexico border since 2001, and that a serious terrorist could likely evade border security or find another mode of entry. Critics also note that approximately half of all undocumented residents entered legally and simply overstayed their visas, that heightened security makes illegal migrants afraid to return home and thus more likely to settle permanently, and that the workers are so desperate (and the smuggling industry so lucrative) that people will continue finding new ways to get through. Although migration has indeed decreased in newly fenced areas of the border, it has simultaneously increased in more remote areas, causing hundreds of migrants to perish from heat exposure and dehydration in the desert each year. In fact, total illegal border crossings have continued at a fairly steady rate since the 1990s, despite a five-fold increase in U.S. spending on immigration enforcement during that time. (In response to this trend, the Bush administration advocated a policy of increased border enforcement combined with a guest-worker program, to provide a legal route for immigrant workers to enter the country. See Agricultural Guest-Worker Programs box, page 39.)

Other controversial aspects of the border fence include:
- **Land acquisition.** In some areas, the border is lined with homes, businesses, and recreational and historic sites that will be destroyed to build a wall.
- **Environmental impact.** A fence would cut through federally protected lands such as national parks and wildlife refuges, blocking threatened

and endangered animals from their only source of fresh drinking water and from crossing the Rio Grande to mate. (Although certain portions of the fence will have holes for the passage of small animals, a recently released environmental stewardship plan by U.S. Customs and Border Security still predicts adverse impacts on wildlife due to habitat fragmentation.) While illegal immigration also harms the environment by generating trash and making trails through the desert, many believe the impact of a wall would be worse.

- **Waiving of federal laws.** The REAL ID Act of 2005 allows DHS to waive any federal laws in order to expedite the construction of border barriers. Chertoff has already waived more than thirty laws (including the National Environmental Policy Act, Endangered Species Act, Clean Water Act, and Wilderness Act) in order to continue construction along the border.

- **Impact on native lands.** The proposed fence would divide the two halves of the Tohono O'odham reservation, where people cross the border regularly to visit a tribal health center, attend school, and visit ancestral camping grounds. While immigration already burdens the tribe (costing millions of dollars per year for emergency medical care to migrants, trash cleanup, and police services to deal with aggressive smugglers and drug dealers), many residents believe that a fence poses its own threats, such as isolation of communities and increased harassment by border patrol agents.

- **Failure to address the underlying issues.** U.S.-Mexico migration stems from a lack of income-earning opportunities in Mexico and a demand for migrant labor in the U.S. The Immigration Policy Center recommends a new policy that acknowledges the contribution of migration to both nations' economies and the need for security cooperation to approach terrorism as a North American rather than solely U.S. issue, and for an investment fund to boost environmental protection and economic development in Mexico. Mexican president Felipe Calderón has supported such an approach, stating that "the wall will not solve any problem. . . . [I]t is much more useful to solve common problems and foster prosperity in both countries."

(See reference section for source material.)

We stop next at Valle Vista, a small colonia on the U.S. side of the border. Here, colonias are defined as any residential areas that lack basic infrastructure such as potable water, sewage systems, electricity, paved roads, and adequate housing. They too sprang up in the 1980s, in response to a housing shortage for farm laborers and other low-income workers in Texas and New Mexico. Developers bought up cheap land in the desert and divided it into lots, creating unincorporated subdivisions with no regulatory oversight. These lots were sold to very low-income people, mostly of Mexican descent and employed in agriculture or construction, who erected makeshift shelters and gradually built homes as they could afford materials. The older colonias like this one tend to have more durable and established housing, although a lack of proper drainage and sewer systems still contributes to high rates of illnesses such as dysentery and hepatitis.

From where we stand, Valle Vista is just a grid of unpaved streets lined with trailers and houses, sandwiched between the train tracks and a road to the nearby landfill. Our guide Verónica, who works with an organization called the Colonias Development Council, tells us briefly about the controversy over the landfill. The U.S. is held responsible for all waste generated by the maquiladoras, she says, so this landfill handles waste from El Paso and from the Juárez maquiladoras as well. About four hundred dump trucks drive past this subdivision daily, beginning long before dawn, yet apparently the lots were sold without buyers knowing it was next to a landfill!

As Verónica describes it, the borderlands are "the backyard" of both the United States and Mexico, a place where factories and landfills alike have contaminated the environment and caused an array of serious health issues. It doesn't really matter which side of the fence you live on; the borderlands are a territory unto themselves, a place where the words "environmental racism" seem to be written everywhere, like invisible graffiti.

Cervantes Enterprises Inc., a large chile pepper operation in New Mexico, which employs migrant workers in its fields on both sides of the border

Our tour moves away from the border now, through a rich neighborhood of mansions and SUVs and manicured lawns, a bizarre bubble of wealth here in this poverty-stricken region. (Eric attributes such opulence to the presence of a nearby casino, vineyards, and drug trafficking.) We drive past this town and continue north, through a wide-open plain of cattle feedlots and agricultural fields. Much of the land is actually fallow, having been purchased by urban developers in recent years, despite the fact that there isn't enough water here to support such growth. The Rio Grande is already stretched to its limits, Verónica explains, and urban expansion along the border is sucking up groundwater much faster than it is naturally replenished.

We finally arrive at the headquarters of Cervantes Enterprises, Inc., a company that grows and processes chile peppers here in New Mexico. We gather around the lobby and are welcomed by the company's general manager, Dino Cervantes, who begins by telling us how his grandfather started growing vegetables on a few fields here in this desert valley back in the 1930s. This is an ideal climate for growing chile peppers, he says, and, as the nationwide popularity of hot sauce increased in the 1970s and 1980s, the farm shifted its focus to chile peppers, opened a processing plant, and evolved into a large company. Cervantes Enterprises now handles thousands of pounds of peppers per day, mashing them into a paste that's delivered in huge rail tank cars to destinations all over the country and to big overseas buyers such as Saudi Arabia.

The company currently grows peppers on about one thousand acres in the U.S. and three thousand in northern Mexico, a big change since the early 1990s, Dino says, when virtually all of their production took place right here in this New Mexico valley. Like most other chile producers in the area, though, Cervantes has shifted south of the border where it's cheaper to grow.

And the main reason it's cheaper? *Labor.* Chile peppers are a very labor-intensive crop, he explains, and labor can account for up to 60 percent of production costs. This would ordinarily just make peppers a more expensive food to buy, but it isn't so simple. Ever since the signing of the North American Free Trade Agreement (NAFTA) in 1994, the U.S., Mexico, and Canada have been allowing goods from one country to enter other member countries tax free, thereby affecting the prices in those countries' markets. We typically think of this situation as hurting Mexican farmers, Dino says, but it's hurting *his* business in much the same way. Following the signing of NAFTA, imports of cheap Mexican peppers suddenly skyrocketed, driving U.S. chile prices down dramatically. How can Cervantes Enterprises compete with growers in Chihuahua, Mexico, where the minimum wage is just five dollars per day? (Ironically, there's pressure on Mexican producers as well, as they struggle to compete with South America and Southeast Asia, where wages are even lower.)

The root issue doesn't seem to be NAFTA, I think, *but the concept of free trade in general. I understand the economic reasoning behind it, the idea of "competitive advantage," which holds that countries should specialize in the goods they can produce most efficiently while importing those they cannot, in order to improve resource allocation and provide consumers with higher-quality products at lower prices. Advocates of free trade claim this brings greater prosperity to everyone involved, but is anyone asking* **how** *one country is able to produce goods for the lowest price? Is it because they pay their workers slave wages, or because they lack environmental regulations—and if so, are they really the best ones to provide that item to the rest of the world? In a system of unregulated trade, as I understand it, the producer with the cheapest price wins, so whoever cuts the most corners to lower their costs will prevail. What does that mean, in terms of product quality and worker rights and environmental protection? What does it mean in terms of abundant, cheap fuel to ship things around, and the maintenance of stable political relations among trading partners? Can we ever really take those things for granted?*

Labor supply is an issue Dino wants to talk about as well. Even if you were to raise wages, he maintains, there's still a shortage of agricultural labor here. People are increasingly finding work in construction, restaurants, hotels, anything that doesn't require the arduous monotony of fieldwork. Up until the 1990s, he remembers nostalgically, high school students and other locals would come out to pick chile peppers on evenings and weekends as a source of supplementary income, but that doesn't happen at all anymore. Like the migrants, this younger generation would rather steer clear of farm labor. No matter *what* you pay, he says, people are simply unwilling to do this work anymore.

Labor and immigration are clearly topics that Dino has considered at length, as he used to chair the Labor Advisory Committee of the American Farm Bureau Federation and has long spoken out against anti-immigrant policies and sentiments in the United States. "You all have benefited from those people being here," he says, "and the fact is that we need those people in order to keep our economy going. The more time we spend arguing about that, the longer it will take to reach any sort of resolution."

Cervantes employs from around thirty to eighty workers here in New Mexico (depending on the season), and uses a computer system to record hours worked and buckets harvested so that workers are guaranteed at least minimum wage. Dino tells us stories about long-term employees who began by digging ditches, then moved on to driving tractors, and later progressed to maintenance and supervising; one man worked for the company steadily for thirty-eight years and managed to buy a home, save for retirement, and put five kids through college. It sounds to me like this employer has really made an effort to provide good labor conditions, even though the broader economic system limits how much a grower can do while remaining competitive.

Given the current reality of declining prices, foreign competition, and shortage of labor, Dino actually sees mechanization as the only long-term option for survival of the chile industry here in New Mexico. Many producers are already cutting labor costs, he says, by switching to mechanical harvesters. These machines strip the plants bare and allow only one harvest per season (rather than two or three), which decreases land productivity yet greatly increases productivity per unit of *labor*, as one harvester accomplishes the equivalent of forty to fifty workers.

Without mechanization, Dino concludes, chile growers and processors will continue moving to places with cheaper labor, and New Mexico will lose the $400 million, five-thousand-employee chile industry altogether. But if growers agree to mechanize and eliminate those harvesting jobs, at least the processing jobs will remain here, and the industry will survive. Dino has resigned himself to this as the best available option.

Liberating people from monotonous stoop labor seems like a good thing, I muse, *but mechanization has disadvantages as well. It's a huge investment that's only possible for very large farms like Cervantes, it creates more pollution, and it may jeopardize the preservation of many traditional chile varieties due to the development of new breeds for mechanical harvesting. It's interesting to me that Dino sees only two options: a system of agriculture that is mechanized, or one that relies on grueling manual labor nobody wants to do. Given that choice, I can see why mechanization looks like a good idea. But are there really only two options?*

My mind drifts back to several diversified organic farms in the Central Valley of California, where I've been a visitor, volunteer, intern, or employee over the past few years, and where workers typically perform each task for only a few hours before moving on to something else. The workday at such farms is varied, reducing the tedium of stoop labor and the health risks of repetitive stress. Workers often have year-round employment, are included in decision making for the farm, and partake of the food they help grow.[6]

*Under this type of system, I wonder, wouldn't more people be willing to take farm jobs? But of course, that's an entirely different model of agriculture than the one we're seeing here. If New Mexico is to remain the "chile pepper capital of the U.S." (or the world), it will need to maintain those vast mono-cultures of peppers, while importing the rest of its food from vast monocultures in other places. In such a system, Dino Cervantes really **is** limited to only those two options, but in a system of local economies in which farms are smaller, diversified, and serving consumers only in their immediate region, aren't there more possibilities?*

Interestingly, despite his strategy of mechanization, Dino still stresses that "agriculture, in the bottom line, needs a work force." Many aspects of crop production can be mechanized, but there will always be certain parts that require human hands to do the work.

We take a drive out to the pepper fields, past acres and acres of uniform rows and irrigation ditches, a bright green quilt spread across this arid plain. We had hoped to talk with some workers themselves, but it's already mid-afternoon and everyone's gone for the day, so we just take a quick look around the fields and then head back to El Paso.

NAFTA and the U.S.-Mexico Border

Since 1994, the North American Free Trade Agreement (NAFTA) has removed import barriers and facilitated increased trade and investment among the U.S., Mexico, and Canada. All three governments view NAFTA as a success, claiming that it has brought new jobs, higher wages, and greater overall prosperity to their citizens. Yet critics argue that free trade has suppressed wages and caused a net *loss* of jobs, as U.S. factories have relocated to Mexico and farmers in both countries have been forced to compete with cheaper imported products.

The Center for Trade Policy Studies (CTPS) in Washington, D.C., challenges this viewpoint, stating that any loss of U.S. manufacturing jobs has merely been due to a recession in 2001, to declining demand for U.S. imports in East Asia, and to technological advances reducing the need for labor. And in cases in which factories have indeed shut down and relocated to Mexico, CTPS claims this has benefited the U.S. by allowing a shift toward other sectors with better-paying jobs. But opponents of NAFTA maintain that wages and working conditions have actually deteriorated under the trade agreement, as transnational companies routinely violate labor laws and threaten to move overseas if workers demand better treatment.* Although NAFTA's "labor-side agreement" provides a system for investigating reports of such abuses, it lacks any practical means of enforcement to ensure that labor laws are upheld. NAFTA's environmental-side agreement has also received criticism for its ineffectiveness at addressing serious trade-related environmental issues. (Meanwhile, NAFTA's "investor-protection" provisions, which allow corporations to sue a government whose laws or policies limit corporate profits, have been very effective and achieved dramatic results.)**

Nowhere is the controversy over NAFTA's labor and environmental impact more pronounced than in the U.S.-Mexico border region, which has experienced massive population growth and deepening issues of water supply, waste disposal, immigration, drug trafficking, public safety, health, and environmental contamination since the signing of NAFTA. Despite its heavy impact on the region, the trade agreement includes no programs for border development, and has therefore left the resource-constrained cities unable to provide electricity, potable water, sewage, paved streets, schools, health clinics, and other basic infrastructure for their rapidly expanding populations. Residents suffer from preventable diseases such as hepatitis A and tuberculosis (at rates much higher than the rest of the U.S. or Mexico), in addition to high rates of cancer, lupus, and birth defects linked to industrial toxins that have proliferated since the signing of NAFTA.

During negotiations for the trade agreement, U.S. and Mexican government officials argued that NAFTA would help reduce such problems, by generating resources for border environmental cleanup and allowing industry to move southward from the border. Yet despite those predictions, industrial development has remained heavily concentrated in the region, and the two binational institutions responsible for environmental projects have thus far failed to achieve their promised objectives.

According to researcher and U.S.-Mexico border specialist Timothy Brown, the border region has not only been neglected by NAFTA and both governments, but has also been compromised by the existence of a political boundary that makes it difficult to enact cohesive development strategies for the area as a whole. Because the border's millions of residents depend on the same air and water, suffer the same diseases, and live within a matrix of economic and familial ties spanning both sides of the fence, Brown argues for the creation of a binational "trans-border authority" to create regionwide policies and establish a stronger voice in multinational trade negotiations. He also maintains that because of its distinct economic, social, and environmental characteristics, the border should be granted representation as a "fourth member of NAFTA."

---

*A Wall Street Journal survey in 1992 reported that one-fourth of almost five hundred American corporate executives admitted they were likely to use NAFTA as a bargaining chip to hold down wages. In 1996, the North American Agreement on Labor Cooperation (NAALC) commissioned a study (under NAFTA's "labor-side agreement") to evaluate charges by the Communications Workers of America and their Mexican counterpart that U.S. employers were undermining freedom of association and collective bargaining rights by selectively closing plants that were undergoing organizing drives. The study found that 50 percent of private sector employers had indeed threatened to close down or move in response to union organizing campaigns.

**Former chief economist and senior vice president of the World Bank Joseph Stiglitz stresses that the hardships faced under NAFTA are not solely due to free trade but to a lack of regulatory effectiveness (e.g., rigorous inspections to see if labor and environmental standards are being upheld, and penalties if they are not) as well as limited resources to subsidize infant industries and pay for environmental protection. According to Stiglitz, trade must be combined with good policies and well-financed international efforts to promote the well-being of all socioeconomic classes, rather than simply leaving this responsibility in the hands of private corporations and resource-constrained governments.

(See reference section for source material.)

La Mujer Obrera, an El Paso grassroots community development organization through which unemployed former factory workers are revitalizing a neighborhood and creating new economic opportunities for themselves

For lunch, we eat at the Café Mayapán, a project of the nonprofit we'll be visiting this afternoon. The restaurant is located in a renovated warehouse in El Paso's run-down South Central neighborhood, but in contrast to its stark surroundings, the room is bright, spacious, and colorfully decorated with handcrafted furniture and traditional Mayan-style murals.

We learn that this used to be El Paso's garment manufacturing district, home to many brand-name companies like Wrangler and Levi Strauss, and employing the largest concentration of Mexican women workers anywhere in the U.S. But with the passage of NAFTA in the early 1990s, these factories quickly relocated to Mexico and left over thirty-five thousand women here without jobs[7]—without prospects for jobs either, since many were over forty-five years old and didn't speak English. NAFTA promised vocational training and new employment, but those promises never materialized, and many of the displaced workers have joined welfare programs in order to survive. El Paso's poverty rate increased after the departure of the factories, so that nearly half the population now lives at or near the poverty level . . . and most of these people are Mexican immigrant women and their children, living in neighborhoods like this one.

In their minimal efforts to develop this area, planners have tended to exclude the middle-aged Spanish-speaking women, viewing them as a drain on the system and an obstacle to development. So in the early 1990s, a group of former garment workers came together and began formulating their own development strategy to create new opportunities for themselves. The members of *La Mujer Obrera* (the Woman Worker) had already been active for several years, fighting for worker rights and protesting against NAFTA, but at this point they shifted gears and began formulating a new model of development for the old garment district, one that would be locally based, rooted in Mexican culture and heritage, and planned by the community members themselves.

After a deliciously authentic Mexican meal at the Café Mayapán, we meet with Lorena Andrade, one of the coordinators of La Mujer Obrera. She leads us into another part of the building, which houses a small health clinic, a computer lab, a library, offices, and classrooms for learning English and general education. In one of the classrooms we meet Rosando Perez, who was a teacher back in Mexico but came to El Paso and worked in a jeans factory for ten years until he was laid off. Now he teaches here at the center and is helping people get their general education certificates in about six months. At this point, the classroom's library is hardly more than one bookshelf, but Lorena explains her philosophy about naming a new project, even if you don't have all the resources yet. Just give it a name and start building from there, she believes, no matter how small you have to start. After all, La Mujer Obrera began as one tiny office back in the 1990s, and look how much it's grown!

So far, the organization has established several "social purpose enterprises," i.e., businesses that generate profit but serve a social function as well. All the women who manage and work in these businesses are displaced factory workers. At first, if you had asked these women what they knew how to do, Lorena says, they would always reply, "Nothing." Even if they were teachers or weavers or producers of food for their families back in Mexico, the answer was the same: *"Nada."* They'd been taught that whatever they did in the factories and in Mexico had no value, that they themselves were of little value, and this is what La Mujer Obrera is working to change. True development must not address economic needs alone, Lorena believes, but also the need for self-esteem and strong identity.

To achieve such growth, women at the restaurant begin with basic tasks like cleaning, and then gradually move on to serving, cooking, and eventually managing. Even if someone is brand new and just chopping onions, she still attends the general meetings to help make decisions for the organization. And both workers and customers gain knowledge of their traditional culture and cuisine, with new recipes from different regions of Mexico on the menu each week.

Back in the restaurant we meet Elizabeth, who began here as a kitchen helper and is now a manager. After staying for a few years, perhaps she will branch off, as others have, to become a chef or manager somewhere else, or even to start her own restaurant. By working here, she will have gained skills in English, technology, leadership, and business management, as well as a heightened sense of confidence, all of which open doors to other jobs and career paths.

We move next into the adjoining store, El Mercado Mayapán, where traditional art and textiles imported from women's cooperatives in Mexico are on display. Like the restaurant, the store is bright and airy, with beautiful murals painted all over the walls, depicting the history of the El Paso garment workers and their struggle for justice.

"We were laid off by NAFTA," one of the women behind the front counter explains, "so we work here now."

"Are these businesses economically viable?" someone asks.

Lorena says they are, and adds that even if an enterprise must initially rely on grants and outside support, it has a *social* value that must be included in the equation.

Lorena next takes us outside and down the street, to see some of the group's other projects. The neighborhood looks half deserted, with rutted potholed roads and abandoned warehouses . . . a mix-and-match combination of residential housing, vacant lots, empty garages, and industrial plants that have taken up operation in some of the gutted factories. Blatantly absent are local businesses and stores, not to mention recreational facilities such as a community center, library, or park. In general, the whole area strikes me as a bleak, noisy, heavily polluted place to live. But in the middle of all this, La Mujer Obrera has managed

Mexican crafts at the mercado of the women's cooperative, La Mujer Obrera (The Woman Worker) in El Paso, Texas.

to create a popular restaurant, a craft and textile outlet, an attractive low-income housing project of eight small apartments, and also a day-care center that provides affordable after-school child care.

This is true urban redevelopment and revitalization, I think to myself, *yet so different from the city of El Paso's plan for that other neighborhood by the farmworkers' center! Rather than relocating the current residents in order to build multinational big-box stores and unaffordable tract housing, this project is being designed by and for the community members themselves, to create a space that meets their own needs and an economy in which **they** reap the profits.*

By all indications, this project is working. Here in this depressed neighborhood, La Mujer Obrera has successfully developed a few businesses, provided job training and employment, and created a community gathering space and venue for local musicians and artists. It has even attracted tourism, bringing dollars into the local economy.

Has the city of El Paso noticed the success of this model, I wonder, *and has anyone else tried to replicate it?* [8]

Even if such ventures do become self-sustaining in the long run, Lorena explains, it is very difficult to obtain the initial funding to start them. When they sought an investor to start up the child-care center, the group was denied multiple times after consultants learned that it would be run by a group of women factory workers. To get funding, Lorena says, you have to do a feasibility study. But because La Mujer Obrera is experimenting with new models of doing things, they can't prove that a project will be feasible, let alone obtain the funding to carry out such a study. So they just create slowly, one tiny piece at a time, getting support for the next step by showing what they've accomplished so far. The café, which is now six years old, has attracted a strong customer base of South Central residents and business people, as well as university students and tourists, demonstrating that even this depressed area *can* support viable new businesses. But before the restaurant existed, such a thing would have been difficult or even impossible to prove.

Lorena also shows us the empty shell of an abandoned factory down the street, which is the site of La Mujer Obrera's next big project. (Ironically, the current director of the daycare center used to be a worker in this factory.) The vision here is far-reaching: El Centro Mayapán, a 40,000-square-foot warehouse renovated to include local women's microenterprises, stores providing basic goods, a farmers' market, a *tortillería*, a cultural event and meeting space, a media center, and a museum. The center will cater to local residents as well as tourists, and is designed to become financially self-sustaining. But in order to move forward with this project, La Mujer Obrera needs investors willing to support such a project, and also the political will of the city and the U.S. Department of Housing and Urban Development.

For now, the building is a huge gutted shell open to the sky, as the project organizers are still struggling to obtain funding to replace the old roof. But even when describing these challenges, Lorena radiates with confidence and determination. Last week someone advised her that it would be easier to get funding if they didn't mention they were Mexican, she tells the group. "But we are doing this *because* we're Mexican," comes her assertive response, "and because we're women. The factories took our independence, you know? And we want to take it back, whatever that means. . . . We've created enough wealth for everyone else. We're still going to support the community, and bring tourism, and all of that . . . but on *our* terms."

●　●　●

Feeling inspired by the work of this dynamic group, we head back to the farmworkers' center. The rooms are filled with people now, resting on pads and blankets all over the floor, sitting at tables, watching TV. One man sits against the wall, strumming a guitar. It surprises me to see how old some of them seem . . . *grandparent*-age, definitely older than I'd expect for people working long days at stoop labor.

We walk down a hall to the back of the building and gather in a room with a big table, for a meeting with Guillermo Glenn of the Sin Fronteras (Without Borders) Organizing Project. (Sin Fronteras is the umbrella organization that created the farmworkers' center.) Guillermo begins by giving us more background on the labor situation here at the border, much of which he attributes to NAFTA.

"We really don't belong to Texas," he says. "We really exist in this borderland between the U.S. and Mexico." He goes on to reiterate Lorena's story from earlier today, describing how the factories relocated to Mexico overnight and left El Paso to cope with extreme underdevelopment and one of the highest poverty rates in the U.S. Simultaneously, the movement of factories across the border caused rapid population growth and underdevelopment in Juárez as well. All day every day, Guillermo says, trucks filled with goods are lined up crossing the border, a steady flow from south to north, providing all the goods and accessories we take for granted—TVs, toys, clothes, appliances, electrical cables, computers, cell phones. . . . Some say this brings jobs and money into Mexico, but Guillermo explains how it's not a stable or reliable source of wealth. Low-wage *maquila* jobs disappear in the blink of an eye when a company decides to relocate its production somewhere overseas where labor is even cheaper. And besides, the money people earn in the factories doesn't even stay in their communities. Guillermo tells us how maquila workers get seventy-two-hour visas to cross into El Paso on Saturday nights and spend their money here, and how the whole downtown of El Paso depends on these Juárez shoppers.

"We're living off the chaos in Mexico," he says.

While NAFTA allows all these jobs and products to cross the border easily, Guillermo points out, it includes no provisions for the movement of labor. He believes that legalization of workers would help the border economy and allow everyone's wages to increase, yet he questions whether that would actually be enough. "Even if you do legalize," he asks with a shrug, "what are those people going to do? Be slaves, like they are now?" Guillermo wants to take the discussion beyond mere legalization, to look instead at our whole economic system and the

Maquiladoras

The maquiladora industry began in 1965, when the Mexican government established a 2,000-mile-long "free trade zone" along the U.S.-Mexico border. Within this zone, foreign companies could set up factories, import parts and machinery tax free, hire Mexican workers to assemble the goods, then reexport the finished products to the U.S.—with taxation only on the value added in assembly (rather than taxing the full value of the goods themselves). Many large companies such as Sony, General Electric, Ford, Fisher Price, and IBM have set up maquiladoras in order to take advantage of these tax exemptions and Mexico's low-wage labor force. In 1994, NAFTA extended that "free trade zone" to the entire country, but most factories remained concentrated in the border region with close proximity to U.S. markets. The industry grew rapidly through the 1990s and peaked in 2001 with over thirty-five hundred factories and 1.2 million workers, mostly young women who had migrated from rural areas of Mexico to take the new factory jobs. Although lower wages in Asia and Central America have prompted many companies to relocate in recent years, thousands of factories have also continued to operate in Mexico, employing close to one million people and producing everything from shoes and toys to electronics, tools, and household appliances.

Proponents claim that maquiladoras have raised Mexico's average income and provided valuable jobs and independence to women workers, while critics draw attention to the industry's poverty wages, lack of independent unions, high rates of sexual harassment and violence, severe pollution of the border region, dangerous and unhealthy working conditions (causing respiratory and skin disease, cancer, musculoskeletal disorders, and other health issues), and substandard living conditions. Because the companies are exempt from paying local taxes, border cities lack funding to provide for their growing populations, and workers have been forced to erect makeshift shelters in sprawling slums without electricity, potable water, sewage, garbage collection, or adequate roads. Moreover, a recent study found that maquiladora wages are insufficient to meet workers' basic needs, and that it would require four to five such minimum-wage salaries to support a family of four in the border region.

These conditions persist despite the fact that the Mexican Constitution has some of the highest labor standards in the world, and despite NAFTA's so-called labor side-agreement, whereby citizens can submit complaints if a government fails to enforce its own labor laws. The investigation process under this agreement takes years and produces mere recommendations with no method of enforcement, while Mexico's heavy reliance on foreign investment dollars makes it nearly impossible for the government to pressure foreign companies to uphold its labor laws.

Nevertheless, grassroots citizen action on both sides of the border has, in some cases, successfully advanced worker rights in the maquiladoras. In the border city of Piedras Negras, garment workers created their own clothing manufacturer and wholesaler, where they now pay themselves double the standard wages of the large maquiladoras. In 2001, the United Students Against Sweatshops organized a widespread boycott against Nike, pressuring the corporation to ensure better pay and working conditions at one of its clothing suppliers in Puebla, where workers had faced firings, threats, blacklisting, and beatings for attempting to start an independent union. Nike also pressed the Puebla state labor board to hold union elections for the factory, and several months later, the company signed a contract with one of the few independent unions ever to exist in a maquiladora. However, these gains are relatively small and isolated cases in the scheme of the maquiladora industry, and in the overall scheme of mass manufacturing and globalized labor.

(See reference section for source material.)

quality of life it offers wage laborers in general. Economic globalization is exploiting people and sucking resources from one place to another, he feels, and the ultimate solution has to be localization, the building of self-sustaining communities.

Eric agrees, saying that the purpose of our trip is to go beyond the standard immigration debate of whether to legalize undocumented migrants, create new guest-worker programs, build a fence, and so forth, and instead to discuss the bigger picture and ways that citizens of both countries can address the underlying issues our governments are ignoring. On that note, Guillermo gives us an overview of his own work with the Sin Fronteras Organizing Project. This effort began in 1983, when a group of local activists visited nearby farms to observe the labor conditions. They began taking action to support the farmworkers in a fight for higher wages and basics like toilet paper and drinking water on the job, and have continued as major proponents of farmworker rights in the border region. Many Sin Fronteras activists are farmworkers themselves, including six of the seven members of the board of directors. Their goals are not only to meet the immediate needs of workers and their families, but also to make fundamental changes to our agricultural system, so that it no longer relies on an underprivileged and exploited labor force.

One of Sin Fronteras' most important victories was the construction of the farmworkers' center in 1994. Guillermo hopes the center will someday be expanded to include a daycare and library, as well as better accommodations for workers. He talks about the obstacles to activism here, explaining how the Mexican government, maquila associations and drug cartels all work together to protect a massive, exploitative system of production in the border area. That's a hard crowd to stand up against, a difficult stage on which to incite change.

While it may be tough to organize here in the borderlands, I'm curious about the idea of organizing in *other* parts of the country in order to support people here. "Do you think boycotts on maquila products are a useful strategy?" I want to know.

Guillermo isn't sure. The national May 1st boycott earlier this year didn't work very well, he says, because people just went shopping and stocked up on everything the day before. Eric adds that boycotts have potential but are usually more effective when the workers are visible to consumers, not hidden out of view in another state or country.

Isn't that exactly the situation that globalization creates? I think to myself. *When the production and the consumption of goods take place thousands of miles apart, how can we maintain accountability between producers and consumers, or true awareness of what our dollars are supporting?*

As we leave the center, I keep thinking about something Eric said earlier today at lunch. In order to create a true democracy, he said, we must have "informed engagement and constructive resistance" on the part of the public. As far as I can see, La Mujer Obrera and the Sin Fronteras Organizing Project are good examples of that, but they are working in a city where very few people even vote, where most residents are struggling to put food on the table and don't have *time* to fight for another world. How to get from this scenario to the ideal Eric described? It's been a long day and I'm tired, but my mind grapples with the question. It's something I'll continue thinking about for the rest of the trip.

July 31st

The next day, we cross the border and travel south through the vast rugged desert of northern Mexico, about two hundred miles south from Ciudad Juárez to the city of Chihuahua. During the bus ride, I record the following thoughts in my notebook:

The land here is flat desert scrub, bare, jagged peaks of red-brown rock, jutting into an endless blue sky patterned with giant cloud formations. In some places the mountains are close and in others distant, and sometimes the land just stretches on and on forever, clouds and scraggly desert vegetation getting smaller and smaller until they blend into a hazy line in the distance. Other than the road and train tracks and power lines stretching north to south, this part of the desert bears no obvious human intrusion. It's just a thousand subtle shades and shadows, an immensity of land and sky and sun.

The idea of a border out here seems strange, because it has nothing to do with the land. No mountain range or huge wide river, no change of climate. . . El Paso/Juárez is one sprawling binational city that continues on both sides of the Rio Grande. The border checkpoint was just a brief stop on our way through that giant metropolis, and now the scenery appears similar to any other Southwestern desert. I have to keep reminding myself "This is México!" just for the novelty of the realization, and because otherwise I'd forget.

I have seen with my own eyes that the border is a human construction, a belt of pollution and economic depression resulting from decades of skewed government policies and neglect . . . a region that provides for the rest of North America yet neglects its own citizens . . . a stage on which NAFTA's deadly side effects play out largely unnoticed by the rest of the world. This is what **we** *have created here, I think to myself. A region whose history and future are defined by the existence of a line, a fence that separates nothing distinct to the immediate north or south. If you erase humans and look only at the land, the border means nothing. It doesn't even exist.*

2

Chihuahua

*Meeting with farmers' organization El Frente Democrático Campesino
and Chihuahua state representative Victor Quintana to learn about
the history of migration from this agricultural region*

On the bus, we pass a couple of small towns and agricultural fields, unexpected patches of green in the middle of this seemingly endless desert. I've been reading a book called *The Devil's Highway* by Luis Alberto Urrea, a true story of fourteen migrants crossing the Arizona desert northwest of here, and perishing from heat exposure and dehydration. Looking out the window as we drive along, I try to imagine being out in that desert with nothing but a small water bottle and backpack, walking for days in the blistering sun with nowhere to take shelter. I imagine the hundreds of human skeletons scattered throughout this land, all the uncounted bodies that will never return to their loved ones waiting back home. People in Mexico are well aware of the rising death rate, yet they continue streaming north anyway, which makes me wonder what we are going to find in the communities we visit here, what level of desperation that would compel people to knowingly take such a risk. I wonder if we'll meet returned migrants who have made that journey themselves.

After several hours rolling through the flat, parched wilderness, we suddenly arrive in Chihuahua City. It's too much to take in, after all that desert, this abrupt shift into a world of crowded streets, traffic horns, billboards, old adobe and brightly painted walls, vacant lots of rubble, tall buildings, hanging laundry, concrete, muddy rainwater, scrawny sidewalk trees, Coca Cola logos everywhere you look, pictures and signs and words crammed onto every surface. A whirlwind of color. I no longer have to remind myself that I'm in another country.

We have lunch at a restaurant in the city with leaders from *El Frente Democrático Campesino*, the Farmers' Democratic Front. This organization was formed back in the 1980s, when farmers from throughout the state of Chihuahua began protesting the government's withdrawal of support for small producers and demanding a higher price for their crops. Here to tell us more of that history are Rogelio Ruelas (a farmer and local leader of the Frente) and Victor Quintana (a long-time advisor to the Frente and a representative in the Chihuahua state congress).

Dr. Quintana begins by giving us a condensed history of twentieth-century Mexican agriculture and politics. Following the Mexican Revolution in the early 1900s,[1] he says, there was a lot of government support for agriculture. This included redistribution of land to peasants, credit programs for farmers to start new productive projects, and restrictions on imports in order to protect the domestic production of goods.[2]

According to Dr. Quintana, during a period from the 1930s through the 1960s, agriculture thrived and migration was very low. Even when the U.S. introduced the Bracero Program in 1942 to recruit thousands of seasonal "guest workers" from over the border, Mexican farmers mainly used it as a temporary income-earning opportunity, returning afterward to their own farms in Mexico. When the Green Revolution began in the 1940s, he says, Mexico was actually at a high point of agricultural production and was self-sufficient in its grain supply.

According to Dr. Quintana, the crisis for small- and medium-scale farmers really began with the national debt crisis of 1982. Mexico had taken out massive loans from international banks over the previous two decades, mainly to develop its petroleum industry. But a drop in oil prices, worldwide recession, and rising interest rates in the early 1980s made it impossible for many Latin American nations to keep up with their loans, and in 1982 the Mexican government announced a temporary moratorium on debt payments.

In response, the World Bank and IMF[3] intervened, restructuring Mexico's debt so the country could once again resume payments. In exchange for such assistance, the government was required to implement "structural adjustment programs," a strategy for generating new

Origins of the Green Revolution in Mexico

The term *Green Revolution* refers to a major effort during the 1960s and '70s to introduce modern agricultural science (i.e., mechanization, chemical fertilizer, and improved crop breeds) to traditional and peasant farmers around the world. This project was based on a popular belief that world population would soon outstrip food production, and that the only way to end hunger and avert widespread famine was to increase agricultural productivity.*

The precursor to this "revolution" took place in Mexico during the 1940s, with the policies of President Avila Camacho and sponsorship from the Rockefeller Foundation, a U.S. philanthropic organization based on the profits from John D. Rockefeller's Standard Oil Company. The foundation had already established a public health project in Mexico decades earlier and, in 1941, sent a survey team of three U.S. scientists to investigate the potential for an agriculture project as well. These scientists recommended a program to train Mexican agronomists, improve weed and pest control, and breed higher-yielding varieties of maize, wheat, and beans. They suggested an initial focus on large commercial growers, with later expansion to reach small-scale peasant agriculture.

Such recommendations contradicted those of UC Berkeley geography professor Dr. Carl Sauer, who had a great deal of experience and knowledge of the Mexican countryside, and whom the foundation had also sent to review Mexican agriculture. Sauer recommended a primary focus on the needs of peasants, noting that their agricultural and nutritional practices were "excellent" and that the main problems were economic (for example, isolation from markets and lack of access to credit) rather than cultural or agricultural. But unlike the other scientists, Sauer's evaluation generated little discussion among members of the foundation.

In 1941, two foundation officials met with then-U.S. vice president Henry A. Wallace and stated that one of Mexico's most important problems was the need for greater agricultural production. Wallace too expressed concern about low productivity in the face of a high birth rate, and encouraged the creation of the Mexican Agriculture Program (MAP) as a joint effort between the Rockefeller Foundation and the Mexican government. MAP established crop research stations throughout Mexico, where scientists began collecting the highest-yielding strains of corn and wheat (from within Mexico and abroad) and cross-breeding them to create new varieties with greater disease resistance and higher yield. Over time, the scientists bred varieties capable of responding to high doses of fertilizer and—when grown on irrigated land under favorable conditions—yielding far more than traditional varieties.

Over the following two decades, Mexican agricultural production grew tremendously and the country became self-sufficient in its grain supply. However, this success was not solely due to chemicals and higher-yielding crop varieties, but to government policies supporting domestic agriculture and ensuring affordable food for the entire population. Self-sufficiency was not simply the result of greater *quantities* of food being produced, but of government intervention and programs making sure everyone had *access* to food.

This changed during the 1970s, when, in response to a growing demand for meat by the urban middle and upper class, the government prioritized the production of feed-grains (for livestock) over that of food grains (for human consumption), and the availability of basic grains as a food source began to decline. Even though agricultural growth had made it possible to provide 2,623 calories and 80 grams of protein per day to the entire population, an estimated one-third of Mexicans in 1970 (mainly in the countryside or in migrant settlements just outside cities) still could not obtain an adequate diet and suffered from malnutrition. This illustrated the project's failure, in spite of increased productivity, to actually reach the poorest segments of society.

Today, critics of the Green Revolution argue that the so-called food shortage of the early 1940s was itself the result of inadequate policies and distribution rather than low productivity. It's clear that the urban demand for food in the early '40s was growing faster than total output, prices were rising, and a short crop of corn in 1943 led to public protests and riots throughout the country. But according to Cynthia Hewitt de Alcántara of the UN Research Institute for Social Development, this was not the result of a lack of agricultural capacity so much as a "sudden shift in consumption priorities at the turn of the decade." Alcántara asserts that production in the countryside had actually been increasing and that food was plentiful, but that it would have taken time and investment to build the infrastructure for channelling that production to urban consumers. The proponents of industrialization, however, were unwilling to provide such investment to smallholder agriculture. As a result, the majority of food entering the national market during the 1940s came from large commercial farms, while vast numbers of smaller growers remained isolated from markets they might have supplied.

Because no major inventory of total domestic food production appears to have been taken at the time, it is difficult to prove whether production at the outset of the Mexican Agriculture Program was in fact adequate to meet the needs of the country's population. The founders of MAP simply assumed that food shortages resulted from the limits of agricultural production, and that modern technologies would raise yields and thus solve the problem. But the debate over the necessity of those technologies, and their social and environmental impacts, continues today.

---

*For an excellent in-depth discussion of the origins and motivations of the Green Revolution, see chapters 6, 8, and 9 of Angus Wright's *The Death of Ramón González* (Austin, TX: University of Texas Press, 2005).

(See reference section for source material.)

revenue (to repay debts) by increasing exports, attracting foreign investment, and cutting spending in areas such as social services and agriculture. So Mexico's agricultural programs—crop research, grain marketing and distribution, price supports, and loans for farmers—were drastically reduced or eliminated altogether.

Then, when Mexico signed the General Agreement on Tariffs and Trade (GATT)[4] in 1986, a flood of foreign goods began entering the domestic market, and the country rapidly shifted from one of the most closed economies in the world to one of the most open. While this expanded trade benefited some large commercial growers in the north by giving them access to foreign markets, Dr. Quintana says it did nothing for peasant farmers throughout most of the country. Mexico became more and more reliant on cheap imported grains, with which its own small farmers (lacking irrigation, large-scale machinery, or government subsidies) could not possibly compete. Such policies, says Dr. Quintana, have dismantled the Mexican countryside, contributing to such high rates of migration that many communities don't even have enough young people left to form a baseball team.

"For every container of corn the U.S. exports to Mexico," he says, "Mexico sends back two undocumented workers."[5]

Rogelio speaks from his own experience, retelling Dr. Quintana's story in simpler terms: "Before the 1980s, our agriculture went well. But once the government started making international trade agreements, we couldn't compete."

I'm curious whether this scenario is starting to change, as the demand for biofuels (from corn ethanol) causes grain prices to increase.

*Suddenly there's a market for all that surplus corn in the U.S., I think to myself, and even a concern over grain **shortages**, as land is switched over to agrofuel production! So does this mean the flow of cheap U.S. corn into Mexico is going to dry up? And based on what we've been hearing, wouldn't that be a good thing for Mexican farmers?*

The topic soon comes up, when Marilyn asks what Rogelio thinks about biofuels in relation to the situation of farmers here.

"It has advantages," Rogelio replies, "but we oppose corn ethanol for Mexico, because you are preferring fuel over food. The amount of corn needed for one tank of ethanol could feed a Mexican family for an entire year. And besides, the production of corn for biofuel is not designed for small-scale farmers in the hills, but for giant industrial monocultures on the plains, using a lot of chemicals. It isn't going to help the land or the *campesinos*."

Dr. Quintana says that he is open to the idea of small-scale biofuel production for local use, but not the corporate, export-oriented model currently being proposed.

"What do you believe should be done about the immigration issue right now, given the current situation?" another person asks.

"Migrants should be entitled to all social and civil rights wherever they are working," Rogelio replies, "and the Mexican government should reinvest in family farming and rural communities, to help people stay on their land."

"We're in favor of an open market," Dr. Quintana adds, "but we have to be prepared for it. Our government didn't prepare us. When the European Union opened its markets, the playing field was first leveled among all the countries, so that their economies were more or less equal."

I mull over this idea in my mind. *Yes, if trade barriers **are** to be removed, the participating countries should be on equal economic footing. Obviously, trade among the countries of Western Europe, or between the U.S. and Canada, is a completely different ballgame than trade between the U.S. and Mexico (as evidenced by the massive migration of workers in the latter case, but not the former). And obviously, the inequalities on the ground must be addressed in order to stem migration and create true prosperity. . . .*

But I'm wary of development that seeks to level the economic playing field

Biofuels in Mexico

Biofuels (typically ethanol or biodiesel) are derived from recently living organisms such as plants, and when produced from agricultural crops such as corn, sugarcane, or palm oil, they are more correctly termed *agrofuels*. Recent growth of the agrofuels industry has been controversial, with supporters promoting agrofuels as a clean and renewable energy source, while skeptics raise concerns that widespread agrofuel production will cause further environmental damage, exploit citizens of the Global South, and lead to food shortages by competing for cropland.

In Mexico, where corn is the dietary staple and primary source of calories for the majority of the population, agrofuels, particularly corn ethanol, have incited much debate. In April 2007, the Mexican Congress passed the Biofuels Promotion and Development Law, which President Calderón later vetoed due to its focus on maize and sugarcane production, in which he claimed Mexico could not compete on a global scale. (Corn-based ethanol production is also very inefficient, requiring large government subsidies and vast energy inputs for negligible net gain.) President Calderón called for a bill with greater emphasis on other crops (as well as algae and cellulosic biofuels), and for more involvement from the Ministry of Energy in addition to the Ministry of Agriculture.

Meanwhile, the private sector in Mexico is already active in biofuels production. In February 2008, the government announced that it would begin issuing permits to energy companies to produce biofuels, in an effort to cut vehicle emissions and boost farmers' incomes. Focusing on beets, yucca root, and sorghum, the Ministry of Agriculture plans to produce three million metric tons of biomass for agrofuels by 2010. But President Calderón has continued to express caution, maintaining that agrofuels have contributed to rising food prices and that Mexico should look to new fuel technologies that do not use food crops.

Proponents claim that agrofuels would help replace Mexico's declining crude oil reserves, and would promote development in rural areas by driving up demand for agricultural commodities. After all, if the U.S. corn surplus were diverted to ethanol production, and exports to Mexico slowed, wouldn't this present an opportunity for small farmers to begin selling their crops in the national market once again? According to analysts at the Americas Program of the Center for International Policy, it isn't so simple. Because millions of Mexican farmers have already left the countryside, and their production systems (i.e., basic equipment, rural mills and storage facilities, distribution channels, and local markets) have been largely dismantled, it would take a large investment for these people to return to the countryside and begin farming again. But based on current trends, it is unlikely that the government or private investors would be willing to finance such a return for small farmers. Moreover, rising land prices due to the demand for agrofuels may prompt even more farmers to migrate and lease their lands to agribusiness corporations, as is currently happening in many places throughout the Global South.

The consolidation of power in the food industry also makes it difficult for small farmers to reenter the market. Large corporations such as Cargill, Gruma, Monsanto, and Archer Daniels Midland have come to own the majority of seed and input suppliers, mills, processing plants, and distribution networks for both food and agrofuels, and it's simpler for these corporations to work with large-scale producers than with peasant farmers. So even with a greater demand for their corn, small farmers may be unable to get that corn onto the market. (And meanwhile, they too will be *purchasing* food at higher prices!) This leads Sitna Quiroz of the U.K.-based Overseas Development Institute to conclude that unless the underlying problems of land distribution and marginalization of small farmers are addressed, agrofuels will continue to have a negative impact on the Mexican countryside.

(See reference section for source material.)

*for the primary purpose of opening up trade. Would this mean bringing Mexico to the same level of per capita resource consumption now practiced in the U.S (a level that could not possibly be sustained worldwide, and that has brought plenty of its own problems such as pollution, depletion of groundwater, obesity, reliance on cheap foreign labor, etc.)? This seems to be what many economists view as the natural course of development, but based on what I've seen so far, it doesn't make sense. Like Dr. Quintana, I wholeheartedly support the goal of reducing rural poverty in Mexico, but **not** for the purpose of global trade! Ultimately, as I understand it, unregulated trade puts small producers into competition with the rest of the world, and whoever has the lowest price wins—even if that "winner" is paying slave wages and located halfway around the world! Without some form of deliberate and active regulation, this sounds to me like a fuel-intensive race to the bottom.*

Meeting with farmers in the small town of Santa Isabel, Chihuahua, to hear their experiences and perspectives on migration

After lunch we drive out into the countryside, through green agricultural fields and arid hillsides of cactus and twisted ocotillo, to the small town of Santa Isabel, where some farmers from El Frente Democrático are to meet this afternoon. We gather in a small local auditorium with a school cafeteria feel, where chairs and benches are set up in rows for the meeting and several dozen people stand around talking informally. It seems that everyone is middle-aged or older, with graying hair and weathered hands . . . the men all in stiff cowboy hats, plaid shirts, jeans, silver belt buckles and leather boots, the women wearing blouses, skirts, and head scarves. They sit in small groups, talking quietly, and I wonder if these are the wives of other people here, or if they have come to fill in for husbands who are gone.

The meeting begins and Eric stands to introduce our group, saying we have come to learn about the reality of the campesinos, which most in the U.S. know nothing about. People there don't understand why so many immigrants are crossing the border, he explains, and this has resulted in a lot of discrimination. So we would like to learn firsthand, from the perspective of everyone here, why so many are leaving.

At first, no one speaks. Eric asks if anyone who has a relative in the United States will raise a hand, and every single hand in the room immediately goes up, to surprised murmurs of *"Todos, todos."* Everyone.

"The young people are all leaving," one person says.

"The prices have all gone down, that's the main reason," offers someone else.

At that, everyone starts talking at once, a buzz of voices all around the room. "There's no work . . . all these products are coming in and destroying the markets . . . if they could get a good price they wouldn't leave. . . ."

One farmer stands up and expresses his views vehemently. "The Mexican government is not interested in farmers. We need our government to get out of their offices and understand the countryside . . . our products here can't possibly compete with imports from the U.S.! But our government doesn't recognize they're exporting labor, that those migrants are growing food and building beautiful houses and doing all that good work for rich people . . . and then the U.S. government treats us like criminals. The debate in the U.S. Congress is missing the point. Please take our message back and spread it, so people understand what our reality is."

I am struck by the resentment in this farmer's voice, his anger at the neglect he perceives not only from U.S. policies and international trade agreements, but from his own government as well. As he speaks, it's as though I can hear the decades of unrest among the Mexican peasantry, a reaction to their long history of marginalization and neglect.

Next, the coordinator of the Frente Democrático in this municipality stands up to speak. He says he has four sons in the U.S., in Louisiana and New Mexico, and that without the money they send home, he would have to sell off all his cattle. (He has shifted to raising cattle because the price for beans dropped so low.) In fact, the greatest source of income for this whole community, he says, is remittance money sent home from the U.S. But until several years ago, people could more easily cross the border and work (especially if there were a bad harvest here) and then return home at the end of the season. Now, he tells us, with heightened border security, it's so hard to get into the U.S. that many people don't dare to come back. They take the risk of migrating with their families, of taking small children and grandparents across that treacherous expanse of Arizona desert, then settling permanently in the U.S. As this man describes it, people do not want to leave Mexico but are simply unable to earn a living here with crop prices so low. "Migration is our only escape valve," he says.

Martha, a young woman from our group who works with the National Farmers' Union in Canada, briefly talks about the similar situation faced by small farmers in her home province of Saskatchewan. Foreign competition and lack of government protection have pushed a lot of people off the land there as well, she says. Basically, free trade is threatening smaller-scale farmers everywhere, not just in Mexico.

Rachel stands and asks how migration is affecting the women in the community, and one woman replies that it's harder because she must fill the roles of both mother and father, while another says the remittance money does help to support her children. "The U.S. government is busy talking about putting up a fence," she says, "but no government is talking about how to help farmers get a good price so they won't have to migrate."

"Why don't they make a program so we can go there to work for awhile and then return home?" another person asks. "Why don't they come down and help us start microenterprises?"

We look at each other, wishing for an answer.

I reflect on the billions of dollars spent by Border Patrol to fortify the U.S.-Mexico border, and wonder what might happen if those dollars were instead spent on loans to farmers, so they could improve their agri-

Agricultural Guest-Worker Programs

People at the meeting in Santa Isabel asked why the U.S. government won't create a program for migrants to work temporarily and then return home. In fact, such a system *has* existed for over fifty years, but it is rarely used. The H-2A program allows an unlimited number of foreign workers to fill temporary or seasonal farm jobs in the U.S., provided that employers first attempt to recruit domestic workers and prove they are unavailable. Employers must also provide H-2A workers with roundtrip transportation, free housing, minimum wage, and other benefits such as workers' compensation insurance.

But the H-2A program is unpopular with both farm labor advocates and agricultural employers, because of inadequate protections for workers and extensive paperwork that makes the program very difficult to use. As a result, enrollment has always been low (approximately 5 percent of all hired farmworkers in 2006), while hundreds of thousands still risk their lives to cross the border illegally for work.

In recent years, the U.S. government has attempted to create a more effective guest-worker program. Pending before the 110th Congress are several bills (including the Agricultural Job Opportunity, Benefits and Security Act, or AgJOBS) to reform the H-2A program by streamlining the process of importing workers, setting higher requirements for wages and working conditions, and offering permanent residency to those who have already worked in the U.S. for several years prior to the new legislation. AgJOBS has been proposed in 2003, 2005, and 2007, but has been highly controversial and thus has failed to pass through Congress. Supporters of a new guest-worker program believe it would reduce illegal immigration, while opponents worry that too many workers would stay in the country illegally after their authorized period of stay. Many also argue that the abundance of foreign labor would continue to drive down wages and conditions, making U.S. workers unwilling to take those jobs.

One way to predict the impact of an expanded H-2A program is to examine the Bracero Program (1942–1964), which brought a total of over four million temporary farmworkers from Mexico to fill the labor shortage caused by World War II. This program ended in 1964 due to the invention of a mechanical cotton harvester, the return of the U.S. labor force, and spreading accusations of worker abuse. The Bracero Program does indeed appear to have reduced illegal immigration during its existence, as INS apprehensions decreased dramatically when it began and rose again after it ended, but limited research on the program also suggests that it lowered wages and domestic employment in some areas, and that exploitive conditions were common.

The question is, what would an expanded and reformed guest-worker program be like today? Even though the Bracero Program received heavy criticism for its treatment of workers, both farm labor advocates and national growers' organizations have shown support for AgJOBS, believing it would do more than past programs to protect immigrant workers' rights.

(See reference section for source material.)

cultural production and start small businesses. I ask myself, *Would that money allocated by Congress to curtail immigration at the border, better fulfill its purpose if spent down **here**?*

"Would it be possible to use that remittance money to make agriculture more economically viable here?" Eric asks them. "What would have to happen?"

"We would still need the government's support," someone says. "And we would need the migrants to return home and help us. We need money in order to build irrigation systems so we can produce more and compete in the market . . . but we also need *people* to do the work."

There actually are a few government programs to help start projects like that, someone says, but they're always changing and have too many requirements and are very hard to figure out. Most of the credit programs are only available to large commercial growers, who produce crops for export and for major food distributors.

Miguel Colunga, one of the Frente leaders who met with us earlier for lunch, explains that beans, corn, milk, and sugar still have some government protection in Mexico right now, but that in January of 2008, NAFTA will enter its final stage and there will be no more barriers to such imports. "Migration will only increase," he says. "We can't stop it entirely, but we could at least reverse the trend, if our government would invest in small- and medium-scale agriculture."

I am now able to see more clearly the role of the Mexican government in the issue of migration. To simply blame foreign corporations or U.S. policies would be inaccurate, since Mexico has long been implementing policies that neglect the countryside. Perhaps those policies are driven by the free trade agreement and the companies that profit from it, but nevertheless, this government made the choice to enter NAFTA and to withdraw support from its small producers. Like all things when you look deeply enough, the situation is complex, and I realize there's no single place to lay the blame.

After the formal part of our meeting is over, people return to chatting in small groups, and I approach Miguel to ask about something I was wondering while listening to the farmers speak. Rather than waiting for the government to provide support so farmers can get better prices in the national market, what about the possibility of working toward self-sustaining communities that produce the things they need for themselves?

Miguel agrees with this approach and says the indigenous communities up in the nearby mountains are like that, growing crops mainly for their own consumption with just a tiny bit to sell on the side. Those communities are more self-sufficient than the commercial farmers down here, and they have lower rates of migration.

This makes me excited. "Do you think it's possible to create something like that in your own communities?" I ask. Miguel says yes, but that it's very difficult, because people rely so heavily on monetary income to pay for things like medical care, clothes, fuel, and other basic supplies.

"Have you done any sort of exchange with the indigenous communities in the mountains, to learn more about how they live?" I want to know.

"Yes, this is one thing the Frente is working on," he says. "We want to create local economies, but it's a big change that will take a lot of time."

I thank Miguel and head outside, where people are still gathered on the sidewalk, talking. I join in one conversation with several of our group members and a local farmer who speaks a bit of English. He tells us about his time as a construction worker in Tennessee, Alabama, Iowa, Louisiana, Texas, and Colorado, and how he used to work for half a year in the U.S. and then spend the other half in Mexico with his family. Now he's older and stays here, but two of his kids live in Dallas. As this man tells stories of his life on both sides of the border, I keep thinking of something Miguel said at the beginning of the meeting: *Tenemos un pie en nuestra tierra y otro pie en el estranjero.* We have one foot in our own country and the other in a foreign land.

August 1st

Visit to El Ranchero Solidario, a rural farmer-owned cooperative grocery store that is creating new market opportunities and providing an alternative to migration

The next day, we head out to the nearby town of Anáhuac to visit a farmers' cooperative. Everyone gathers in a room with rows of desks and a tile floor, the walls bare except for a small crucifix and colorful painting of Christ's resurrection mounted at the front of the room. Rogelio (the farmer and Frente leader we met yesterday) stands and introduces us to Mamá Lolita, a local nun who helps run the cooperative. She is a tiny woman around fifty years old and wearing a headscarf, glasses, a long denim skirt, and a black T-shirt with big white letters saying *La violencia NO es normal*. Violence is not normal. She prefers to be called Sister Lolita, she informs us with a smile, and proceeds to tell the history of *El Ranchero Solidario* cooperative.

Before becoming a nun, Lolita worked in her family's factory. "But God took me out of the factory and put me in the field," she says. "Just like the miracle of the loaves and fishes, in which Jesus distributed food before beginning his sermon, there's a local saying, 'It's better to eat first, and then be a Christian.' The word of God will not stick when you are hungry!" People around the room laugh and nod.

El Ranchero Solidario Co-op in Anáhuac, Chihuahua, which serves 1,000 customers a day.

Rogelio Ruelas and Sister Lolita give a tour of El Ranchero Solidario Co-op.

Many years ago, Sister Lolita says, a local priest and Frente leader named Camilo took her around to the farming communities here, and she told people she had come to serve. One week later, folks started arriving at her door asking for help, because the granaries weren't giving them a fair price for their beans. So she started working with the farmers to organize protests in Chihuahua City, and when people saw her skill at organizing, they invited her to join the Frente. "I've got a lot to say, enough to fill a thick book," she says. "It's my whole life the last twenty years."

With a group of local farmers, Sister Lolita has helped establish a rural grocery store where they can sell their harvest directly to people in the region. Before NAFTA, these farmers used to sell their grain to big companies that would process and distribute it, but then those companies began purchasing cheaper U.S. corn instead. Farmers also used to sell their corn directly to the government, which had a distribution agency that managed the supply and price of staple foods nationwide, but this program was dismantled in the 1980s. As Sister Lolita tells the story, the Mexican government wanted to buy corn for fifty cents per kilo, and people here were fighting for eighty cents. When farmers refused to accept the lower price, the government "got mad and left."

Government Support for Agriculture in Mexico

From the 1930s to the 1980s, the Mexican government played an active role in domestic agriculture and food distribution. The National Food Staples Company (CONASUPO) was established in 1965 to regulate the supply and price of basic staples such as corn and beans. At newly created rural warehouses, farmers sold their crops directly to the government at guaranteed prices, and CONASUPO conducted all the processing and distribution of these goods. It also sold corn cheaply to small private tortilla makers, who could then sell tortillas to the public at an affordable price. Because CONASUPO purchased corn from farmers at high prices and then sold it to consumers at lower prices (with the government paying the difference), this system has been called the "tortilla subsidy." CONASUPO also controlled imports, purchasing corn from international markets in order to build up the country's grain reserves.

In the 1970s, President Luis Echeverría greatly expanded these programs, particularly for smaller producers who had originally been excluded. Echeverría created many new agencies to benefit peasant farmers, with services such as crop insurance, subsidized fertilizer and seed, low-interest loans, and marketing assistance. CONASUPO's budget quintupled, and the agency grew to include thousands of employees, many subsidiary companies, and a large network of retail stores across the country. (However, even these policies favoured commercial growers and did nothing to change the concentration of capital, water rights, and prime land in the hands of a few large farms.) The following administration of José Lopez Portillo continued such policies by creating the Mexican Food System (SAM), which provided farmers with cheap fertilizers and high guaranteed prices, created a rural distribution network managed by community food councils, and provided subsidized "baskets" of basic foods to some nineteen million undernourished Mexicans. This ambitious plan cost nearly four billion dollars in 1980 alone, but did achieve its goal of national food self-sufficiency from 1981 to 1982.

However, like Echeverría's rural development programs, SAM depended on abundant oil revenues and major loans from international banks, and was therefore fiscally unstable. A crash in worldwide oil prices in 1981 left the government unable to afford such generous subsidies to grain farmers, and SAM was abolished in 1982. That same year, the Mexican government declared a moratorium on its debt payments, and the World Bank and IMF intervened with "structural adjustment programs" to stabilize the economy and regain the confidence of foreign investors. Over the next decade, Mexico received many structural adjustment loans and entered several trade agreements, all of which required the government to reduce subsidies, privatize the food distribution system, eliminate guaranteed prices, and boost production for export rather than domestic food supply. (The rationale was that high-value export crops for U.S. markets would generate revenue to import cheap grains, which would meet domestic food needs without the need for expensive subsidies.) As a result, Mexico began in 1982 to gradually dismantle CONASUPO and related agencies. By the mid 1990s, most of the rural warehouses and mills had been either dismantled or privatized, and in 1998 the tortilla subsidy and the last of guarantee prices for corn and beans were eliminated as well. In just over a decade, Mexico shifted from being nearly self-sufficient in basic grains to being a major net importer.

In the absence of CONASUPO, agribusiness corporations such as Cargill, Agroinsa, and Gruma became the primary purchasers, processors, and distributors of Mexican corn. The country's corn industry became highly concentrated in the hands of these few companies, with Gruma (partially owned by U.S. grain trader Archer Daniels Midland) holding 73 percent of the market share. Other transnational food processing firms such as Conagra, Tyson, Unilever, and Nestle significantly increased their operations in Mexico as well, with Unilever taking over CONASUPO's oilseed processing facilities, and Nestle producing virtually all the condensed, evaporated, and powdered milk consumed in the country.

But unlike the government agencies they had replaced, these private corporations did not invest in peasant agriculture or purchase grain from smallholders (which still represented the vast majority of agricultural producers in the country), causing many farmers to lose their market access entirely. (Many smallholders had never actually had access to CONASUPO purchasing offices, but they had still benefited indirectly from the system of guaranteed prices, because it lifted the overall price of corn throughout Mexico.)

During the mid-1990s the government did initiate a few temporary support programs to replace CONASUPO. The Alliance for the Countryside was created to promote a shift from staple crops to agroexports such as fruits and vegetables, and a widespread subsidy program called Pro-Campo was introduced to help farmers transition during the fifteen-year phase-out of tariffs under NAFTA. Rather than setting guaranteed prices for basic grains, ProCampo provided direct cash payments to farmers (both small- and large-scale) based on total acreage. These payments were intended to boost income while allowing farmers to respond to market forces, shifting away from less profitable basic grains and toward agro-export crops. In theory, income subsidies would allow the time and capital for farmers to adopt new technologies, diversify production, and form associations with private agribusiness firms. But in reality, ProCampo payments were inadequate to incite such a change or to help farmers throughout NAFTA's transition period. The program has been unpopular with farmer organizations, which see it as more of a welfare program than true farm policy and resent the government's failure to consult with them in creating it.

Throughout the past two decades, Mexican farmers have actively protested the government's changes to agricultural and trade policy. The National Union of Autonomous Regional Campesino Organizations (UNORCA) continues to demand regulation of basic grains and support for small producers to enter the market. Such support would not necessarily require large bureaucracies and agencies as in the past, but could include basic low-interest loans to diversify production for local markets, and policies to facilitate the formation of farmer-owned cooperatives such as small corn-milling and tortilla enterprises. Based on recent history, however, such a policy shift appears unlikely.

(See reference section for source material.)

After the government withdrew support for domestic agriculture, the farmers here began to organize a co-op, which started small and grew gradually to its present size. Right now there are ten people on the steering committee, twenty-six full-time workers at the store, four part-time workers, and several volunteers. The co-op consists of fifty-two member families, which pay yearly dues and in turn receive a guaranteed buyer for their crop, a good price, and priority status for selling to the co-op. (El Ranchero Solidario sells crops from other producers in the region as well, but only after taking whatever its own members can provide.)

Each year, the co-op does an inventory of thirteen rural communities in the immediate area, to calculate how much is being produced and estimate what they'll be able to sell. They also look at current prices on the Chicago Stock Exchange, because these farmers are still affected by the global market and need to set competitive prices that consumers will be willing to pay. Then the members meet and decide on prices together. With intermediary companies removed from the equation, the co-op is able to offer a better price for both the consumer and the farmer.

To make sure we understand, Sister Lolita gives a hypothetical example. Suppose that companies buy corn for $140 per ton from the farmers, then sell it to consumers at $240 per ton.[6] The companies thereby make $100 profit for every ton of corn sold. But the co-op can buy from farmers at a higher price, like $200 per ton, and sell at a lower price, like $220. Since the store is run by the farmers themselves and isn't a separate business trying to profit, the margin between its buying and selling price can be very small—just enough to cover the costs of operation—and everyone gets a better deal.

Direct Marketing in Agriculture

The situation for farmers in Anáhuac is not unique. In our current globalized food system, the majority of profits are reaped by intermediary companies, not by those who grow food. USDA data show that the costs of transporting, processing, packaging, and distributing foods are growing faster than the prices of crops themselves, so that U.S. farmers who received forty-one cents for each consumer dollar spent on food in 1950 received only twenty-two cents for each dollar spent in 2005. (This actually varies by type of food, from thirty cents for meat and dairy, to twenty-four cents for fresh vegetables, and only six cents for bread and cereal items.) Even with recent spikes in food prices, the portion received by farmers still appears to be falling.

Increasingly, growers are turning to a direct-marketing model in order to bypass the intermediary companies and obtain a higher return for their goods. By selling directly to consumers and thus eliminating the profits of the "middlemen," it's possible to set a better price for both producers *and* consumers. For example, produce at a farmers' market often costs less than at a supermarket, but USDA statistics show that profits to the grower at farmers' markets tend to be higher than profits from selling to wholesalers (who then sell to supermarkets). Other examples of direct marketing include roadside stands; farm-to-institution programs at places such as cafeterias and hospitals; subscription farming, or community supported agriculture; and fair trade cooperatives.

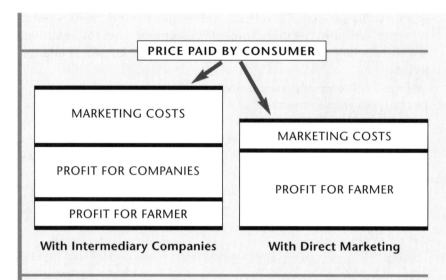

This model applies not only in the U.S., but throughout the world. Coffee farmers, for example, generally receive between thirty and fifty cents for a pound of coffee that may retail for as much as ten dollars. The fair trade movement has begun to address that imbalance by certifying "fair trade" importers that buy directly from farmer cooperatives rather than from intermediary distributors. In one fair trade cooperative in Oaxaca, more than five thousand families have used the additional income for projects to increase their own food security and standard of living, such as health-care services, cooperative corn mills, an agricultural extension and training program, and the region's only secondary school. In India, according to the UN Food and Agriculture Organization, women farmers have built a network of cooperative dairies, raising the incomes of more than eleven million households.

But because most farmers produce raw materials that need some form of processing before consumption, the future growth of this model depends upon the creation of new infrastructure for local, farmer-owned processing. By setting up grain mills, dairy processing facilities, tortilla factories, and storage and/or retail facilities that are owned and run by farmers themselves, these producers will be able to claim a larger share of the value chain, and hence a larger portion of the profits, for the foods they produce.

(See reference section for source material.)

Being organized as a co-op has also given the members more bar-gaining power with companies that wouldn't have dealt with them as small individual producers. Together, they can produce the quantities demanded by such large buyers, although one challenge has been the uniformity required by those companies.

"Has the demand for uniformity caused a loss of diversity in bean varieties grown here?" Martha asks.

"Actually, so many beans are coming from the U.S. that there *isn't* much of a market for our beans here," Sister Lolita replies. "We're mainly producing for the co-op and home consumption, with all the traditional varieties still being grown."

"Are you more food-secure than other people in the area?" Brian wants to know.

Sister Lolita explains that people here grow food for themselves and sell what's left over, so they usually have plenty of food to eat but not enough money to meet other basic needs. But El Ranchero Solidario has provided its members with a more reliable income, she says. Even though it can't always compensate farmers immediately, the co-op will at least sell the crop within a few weeks and then pay a fair price.

This is basically what governing bodies have been doing throughout history in order to make agriculture possible, Eric explains to us. Farming is different from most other economic activities, because yields fluctuate based on temperature, rainfall, and other uncontrollable fac-tors. An auto manufacturer can easily decide how many cars to make, but a farmer can't control how much corn a field will produce in a given year! The auto manufacturer can also make quicker decisions and changes based on market conditions, while the farmer must make decisions at the beginning of the season, invest in a crop, then wait months for it to mature before harvesting and selling. This allows little flexibility in responding to the market, and means farmers must often go into debt to finance their production. In addition, the demand for food (unlike manufactured goods) tends to remain fairly steady, due to a physical limit on how much people can consume. So in abundant years this causes an oversupply on the market, driving down prices and leaving farmers unable to make a living, while leaner years drive prices up and leave many consumers unable to afford enough food.

This is the inherent dilemma of agriculture in a free market. After a good harvest, farmers will naturally put all their grain on the market. (From an individual's standpoint, it's the only logical move: "Everyone else will do it, so prices are bound to be low, so I should just try to sell as much as possible!") As a result, prices fall and the farmers suffer. Because of this natural instability, governments have tended to intervene in agricultural production and distribution.[7] They have created reserves to hold back grain when it's plentiful (in order to keep prices high enough that farmers can survive) and programs to release that extra grain in years of scarcity (to keep prices low enough that consumers can survive). It's that simple. A market left to itself does not perform this function, which is why governments have taken a more active role in agriculture—until recently, when structural adjustment programs and free trade entered the picture and national grain reserves were dismantled, leaving farmers and consumers completely vulnerable to the fluctuations of the global market. But here in Anáhuac, farmers *themselves* are taking on that role abandoned by the government, attempting to moderate their own regional grain supply and prices.

"Are farmers in other areas learning from this model?" Jan asks.

Sister Lolita replies that some people do travel here to see what they're doing, and that just a couple months ago, three truckloads of visitors from the outskirts of Chihuahua City came to learn.

Eric would like to know about the co-op's effect on migration, and Rogelio replies that all fifty-two members and their children have been able to stay here, while many others in this area have been forced to migrate. "People from all over Chihuahua come to buy from our co-op, and that's what has allowed us to stay," Rogelio says. Sister Lolita nods, asserting that coming together and organizing has been the only way to curb migration.

I look around the room and notice a distinct difference between this gathering and yesterday's meeting in Santa Isabel: this time, a few young adults are present and participating in the discussion. There's Rogelio's daughter Lina, who works in the co-op, and a young farmer named Antonio, who belongs to the co-op but used to be a construction worker in Santa Fe, New Mexico. He tells us how the *coyote* (smuggler) charged him one thousand dollars and how he walked for two days and nights without food or water, to cross over the border. After eight months of work, Antonio had earned enough to cover the payment to the *coyote* and to bring a tiny bit of money back home. He says that he will not go back to the U.S., and thanks to the co-op, he probably won't need to.

An older farmer, wearing a John Deere baseball cap, joins in the discussion. "Most of the people who go to the U.S. make more money, but they're not happy. To be happy, you have to be in your own land." A

Local produce at El Ranchero Solidario Co-op.

big problem now, he says, is that Mexico is losing its youth. Much of the young labor force is lost to the U.S., falling prey to debt or drugs, and losing their culture.

But everyone here agrees that the co-op is a source of hope. Several of its original founders have died already, and younger descendents are taking their place. One of the member's sons is a buying agent and manages everything by computer, Sister Lolita says proudly. "They have the seed of cooperativism in them."

After all this talking about the co-op, we are eager to actually see it!

The store is larger than I expected, carrying not only the crops of local farmers but many other products as well. They've contracted with other campesino groups in Mexico and are selling fair trade coffee from Oaxaca, bread and cookies from a nearby Mennonite village, and organic amaranth products from Teotihuacán. The co-op is also making an effort to avoid products that hurt the environment or people's health, Sister Lolita explains, so it does not sell junk food or cigarettes, and even used to have a ban on Coca Cola products, until people rebelled and demanded them back. (*Sounds just like my local food co-op back home!*) Rogelio points out a shelf where boxed instant soups were recently replaced with bags of flour and a sign explaining that processed foods are unhealthy, and that this substitution is merely "a grain of sand in the great struggle to prevent illnesses caused by poor diet."

Other hand-painted signs with positive messages abound: "The cooperative is not a store of profits, but of service." "Organic coffee, for our health and also in solidarity with the *Campesino a Campesino* [Farmer to Farmer] Movement." "More than seeking to cure ourselves, we must seek to stay well. Good health begins with good nutrition."

For all these great principles, though, I'm surprised by the number of mainstream corporate products on the shelves! Deluxe brand cake mix, Smuckers jelly, Yoplait, Nestle, Colgate toothpaste, the infamous Coca Cola. . . . But on the other hand, there's also fresh cheese made by local women, bulk flour and beans grown by the farmers here, eggs and meat from local ranches, fresh fruits and vegetables, and handmade herbal

Sacks of flour in the back room of El Ranchero Solidario Co-op.

remedies. So who am I to judge? Perhaps they need to provide all the other stuff that people want, in order to be successful for now, and perhaps—as that handwritten sign stated—big changes must happen one grain of sand at a time.

The store is usually crowded with more than a thousand customers a day, but this is the one weekday when it's closed, so we get to wander the aisles, and even explore the storage areas where large sacks of corn and wheat flour, all grown by the co-op members, are piled ceiling-high. Rogelio's daughter opens one of the cash registers, and we sample some of their wares (delicious home-baked cookies made from oats grown right around here) before heading out to a farm to see where some of this food is produced.

I'm fascinated to see how the local food movement is happening here in Chihuahua, and it's not a "hippie" or "yuppy" or elitist thing, as it's sometimes perceived in the U.S. This grocery store is not owned by middle-class consumers but by the producers themselves, and it is providing for the basic needs of local people who are by no means affluent. Here, I think, supporting a local food economy is already what it may soon become for all of us—a common people's solution, and a matter of survival.

Visit to a nearby ejido to speak with local farmers and returned migrants about their struggle to start productive projects and make a living in agriculture at home

After thanking everyone and leaving the co-op, we head out to visit Rogelio's *ejido*[8] (small farming community), which produces mainly corn, beans, oats, beef, pork, mutton, and poultry. It's still early afternoon, with sunny skies and patchy white clouds, as we drive along the main road through an expanse of flat green fields. The ejido is located at the edge of this large agricultural valley, nestled into the hills in a rugged landscape of rock and desert scrub. We bump along narrow dirt roads into the small settlement, a scattering of brick houses and fenced corrals and a small stone church, all bordered by walls of intricately stacked stone.

The soil is too wet to be out in the fields right now, and people are gathered around an outdoor fire, roasting *chicharrones* and talking. Rogelio goes over to explain why we've come, while a few of us strike up conversation with two kids of about eleven, who turn out to be Rogelio's younger cousins. They currently live in Mesa, Arizona, and are here to visit for the summer. In the U.S., their mom works at WalMart and their dad is a construction worker, but the family is gradually building a house back home on the ejido, where they hope to return by the time the boys reach high school.

This interests me, since I've been reading about similar scenarios in The Devil's Highway. *Apparently, many people migrate for a specific purpose such as putting a new roof on their home, affording the uniform and text books for a child who's about to start school, buying some cattle, building a house. Loans, when available here, have high interest rates, and the only way most people can afford such a project is to work in the U.S. for a while and save money. From Urrea's book, I've gotten the sense that this motivation for migration is little understood by the U.S. public.*

The boys tell us enthusiastically about how much they like it here, and how they get to help with sowing seed, spreading fertilizer, feeding the animals, riding horses, and driving around in their motor-powered go-cart. They both agree that it's way more fun on the ejido than in Arizona.

"Do you want to be farmers when you grow up?" I ask, but they give me puzzled looks and reply that they already are!

Nearby, people are gathering around in a small circle to talk with a man named Juan Valverde, who recently returned from the U.S. He lived there on and off for eleven years, sometimes with papers and sometimes without. "It's because there is no money here, to do work or to start projects," he says.

Juan tells us about one experience crossing the border, when he sat in Nogales for three days without food, waiting for the *coyote* to take him across. In the U.S., he worked in restaurants, factories, agriculture . . . everything. The last job was as a street cleaner in Denver, Colorado, moving snow off the roads during winter. The hours were sporadic and sometimes went from three o'clock in the morning until eleven o'clock at night. He also has a daughter and son in the U.S., who work in cleaning and construction.

Juan and another farmer here have a project they want to start: putting in a small reservoir for irrigation so they can grow forage crops and produce meat organically. They both saved money while working in the U.S., but it's not enough to start the project, so they want to get a loan of about 150,000 pesos (US$15,000) from the government. Apparently this is very unlikely.

When asked why he wants to grow organically, Juan Valverde replies that it's healthier for the soil and that fertilizers have "ruined" their land. "It used to be that one rain would grow a good crop, but now we can have *fifteen* rains and still not get a good crop," he says.

Eric explains why. The salts and residue components of chemical fertilizer tend to accumulate beneath the soil surface, creating a "hardpan," or layer of compacted soil through which roots cannot easily grow. So after the soil surface has dried out between rains, the plants cannot reach very deep to find water.

Rogelio explains that there's a program in which farmers must raise 40 percent of project costs, and the government loans the other 60 percent. But individual campesinos don't have enough money to cover that percentage, which is why Rogelio believes it's crucial for farmers to pool their resources, form a group, and apply for funding together. He has already begun one such project, using a greenhouse to produce

Effects of Synthetic Fertilizers on Soil

Soil is one of the most important aspects of an agricultural system. Healthy soil absorbs rainfall, allows roots to grow easily, holds water during dry periods, reduces crop disease, and provides nutrients to support plant growth. All these functions take place naturally in soils that have a large amount of organic matter, i.e., any living or once-living material. Just one acre of healthy topsoil may contain 900 pounds of earthworms, 2,400 pounds of fungi, 1,500 pounds of bacteria, and 890 pounds of arthropods and algae! All this organic matter, combined with the mineral portion of the soil (made of pulverized rocks), creates a medium that can support plant growth.

But because agriculture involves the *removal* of organic matter (via the harvested crop), farmers must add inputs in order to maintain the fertility oftheir soil. This is done with organic fertilizer such as compost and manure, or with manufactured fertilizers such as ammonium nitrate and potassium chloride. While the synthetic fertilizers contain the main nutrients required for plant growth (nitrogen, phosphorous, and potassium), organic fertilizers contain those main nutrients along with many other minerals and compounds that sustain microorganisms and thus support all soil life. So even though synthetic fertilizers provide nourishment to plants, they fail to nourish life in the soil. As a result, they provide only an initial boost in yields, while gradually depleting the soil's organic matter and reducing the over-all health and fertility of the system.

Moreover, some fertilizers (especially when accumulated or used in excessive amounts) can directly damage the soil. Some cause a build-up of salts, which impede plants' ability to take up water and nutrients, while others kill microorganisms and cause soil compaction. Farmers commonly report that the long-term use of synthetic fertilizers has degraded the structure of their soil, and that ever-increasing amounts of fertilizer are needed in order to sustain yields from year to year.

But without synthetic fertilizer, would it be possible to grow enough food to sustain the current world population? A 2007 University of Michigan study comparing yields of organic versus conventional food production in 293 cases around the world found that organic methods could indeed provide enough food per capita for the global population (without increasing the area of land under cultivation), and that leguminous cover crops could provide enough nitrogen to replace all the synthetic fertilizer currently in use. At the Rodale Institute in Pennsylvania, nearly two decades of research on experimental plots have found a difference of less than 1 percent between organic and conventional corn yields, with conventional plots taking a much harder hit during the severe drought of 1999. Perhaps most impressive of all, in 165-year-old crop trials at the Rothamsted Research Center in England, organic plots have been found not only to yield higher but to contain six times the organic matter as their conventional counterparts. This growing body of research confirms the existence of viable, highly productive, and ecologically sound alternatives to the use of synthetic fertilizers in agriculture.

(See reference section for source material.)

high-quality forage that can fatten cattle in a short period of only two months. This project is in its early stages and cannot yet support all twenty ejido members who invested in it, but the plan is for them all eventually to be able to make a living off of it.

After talking and looking around for awhile, we climb into the back of Rogelio's pickup truck and ride out to his part of the land, while Eric gives some more background about the ejido system. As we already know, this type of communal landholding was established in the constitution of 1917 (in response to peasant demands for land redistribution during the Mexican Revolution), but it was actually brought to fruition by President Lázaro Cárdenas in the 1930s. Although the state retained legal title to these lands, they were collectively managed by community members and divided for use among their families. The land was legally guaranteed to remain an ejido, and could be passed along to descendants but never sold or leased to outsiders. By the 1990s, just over half of Mexico's arable land had been incorporated under the ejido system. But with recent changes to Article 27 in 1992, people are now allowed to sell or lease ejido land as private property, without ever consulting the rest of the community.[9] Rogelio says there used to be a lot more public works projects here, because everything was cooperatively governed and managed, but now that has changed. Who wants to help with a big project on someone else's fields, if that person might just sell the land and leave?

In Eric's view, the changes to Article 27 were intended to move peasants off the land and into more so-called productive sectors that contribute to the country's exports and GDP.[10] But if that was indeed the government's strategy, he says, it hasn't completely worked. *Ejidatarios* greatly value their land and are hesitant to sell it, even when they migrate. Land provides security, a place to return someday; so despite the government's destruction of the ejido system, many people have held onto their small plots in the countryside.

Rogelio shows us around the ranch and points out several new projects—the greenhouse, a vegetable field, a rainwater catchment system to irrigate

Rogelio Ruelas at La Loma Ejido of Cuauhtemoc, Chihuahua showing his home-grown and milled feedstock used to feed his pigs, cows, chickens and sheep.

apple trees, a barn where the grain harvest is stored and a mill for grinding grain into animal feed. He also takes us to see a pig barn from which the manure is collected in a long cement lagoon, for generating methane gas. This is a cheap and sustainable way that people produce fuel for their homes in some parts of the world, particularly in Asia, and Rogelio has plans to create such a system here on his land.

The afternoon's heavy rain clouds have arrived as they do every day, a dark-purple blanket rolling in from the south, punctuated by frequent streaks of lightning. It's an ominous warning for the coming downpour, and a sign that we should probably get going.

On the way back to Chihuahua City, I sit in the front of the van with Rogelio and our driver, Lino, eager to ask them questions and learn more. In one part of the ejido, we pass a large field of irrigated hybrid corn on one side of the road, across from a field of rain-fed native corn on the other side. The hybrid corn is tall, dense, uniform, and bright green; the native corn smaller, more uneven, and planted farther apart. (Without irrigation, the plants need more space for their roots to spread out and get water.) The hybrid corn is to sell, Rogelio explains, so farmers purchase the seed every year[11] and invest in large quantities of synthetic fertilizer. But on the other side of the road, the native seed is saved and resown every year, with fewer inputs because it's for home consumption.

"Have the two varieties cross-pollinated?" I want to know.

"Yes," Rogelio replies. As evidence, he cites the fact that the native corn has become smaller and less tasty in recent years, and that the plants have lower tolerance for drought, cold, and disease. (While this may be due in part to cross-pollination with the hybrid corn, I'm aware that it might also be due to past overuse of chemical fertilizer and the decline of soil health in general.)

I am struck by the way Rogelio describes this situation so matter-of-factly, as an unfortunate circumstance that he has simply resigned himself to accept.

Aren't there any alternatives, I wonder, *any ways to improve the health and productivity of these fields while staying economically viable? I realize it's complicated; after all, a sudden switch to organic farming could be disastrous in the short term. This soil has become so degraded that it could no longer support a crop by itself, and must now rely upon the synthetic inputs that degraded it in the first place. I know it would take years of hard work to rebuild*

the fertility that's been lost, and that the transition period would cause an ini-
tial drop in yields, so without some sort of support program, how would farm-
ers survive during that transition?

After talking more about the soil and climate and various details about
the ejido, our conversation shifts to the topic of migration. It turns out
that Rogelio himself used to work in the U.S. on and off, for twenty-six
years. He still has relatives in Utah, Nebraska, Colorado, and Arizona,
who are able to move freely across the border because they were in
the U.S. when amnesty was granted, and because some of them have
gotten married. "But there are many other people who want to return home yet get trapped in the U.S.," Rogelio tells me. "They get a
loan for a truck and go into debt, or they get into drugs, and they're
trapped."

By the time we get back to the city, it's pouring rain and the streets
are literally knee-deep in water. The storm drains can't possibly keep up
with such a torrential downpour, and each road has become its own
river. At the street corner near our hotel, a couple of women in long,
brightly colored dresses stand under the shelter of a roadside shop, waiting out the storm. Lino tells me that they are from the *Las Pimas* indigenous group, and that they spend half the year down here in the city,
selling things to people at traffic lights. This surprises me, after what
Miguel said yesterday about the indigenous communities up in the
mountains.

Are they truly self-sufficient? I wonder. If so, why come down here to sell
trinkets at stoplights? Maybe the level of autonomy differs, from place to place,
or maybe things are changing now, or maybe, like the farmers in Anáhuac,
they produce enough food to eat but still need money for other things.

I'm intrigued, and wish we could stay longer and visit those places up
in the mountains.

Sitting around the dinner table later that evening and discussing our
day, several people comment on the remarkable way that El Ranchero
Solidario has managed to carve out a space for itself, despite the difficult economic situation in the countryside. It seems that those farmers
have successfully created an alternative to migration, a regional market
that keeps wealth circulating within their own community. During the
conversation, I hastily scribble these thoughts into my notebook:

*It will never work to just wait for the government to help, to make changes in support of the peasants. Just like the displaced factory workers in El Paso, people will have to organize and build these alternatives themselves, then fight to get the government to just **allow** such things to exist! Successes like we saw today will only come from right here, from the people . . . grass grows from its roots.*

Mexico City

August 2nd

Regional forum of La Vía Campesina, the International Peasant Movement

The next morning we catch a flight to Mexico City, arriving in time for the end of a two-day conference organized by *La Vía Campesina*, the International Peasant Movement. People from small farmer and indigenous groups all over Latin America have come to share their experiences, learn from one another, and discuss efforts to protect the land and resources on which their livelihoods depend. The conference room is filled with people, many of whom appear to be farmers. At least half are women, and several are young adults. It definitely feels like a people's movement. The final meeting of the conference is underway, so I quietly pick up headphones for English translation and take a seat in the back row, notebook ready.

A representative from Brazil is speaking about efforts to educate the children in small settlements throughout the countryside, teaching them about sustainable agriculture so they'll stay on the land instead of migrating someday. She also talks about the struggle to create regional markets, since the settlements are so far apart and transportation is limited.

It occurs to me that rural communities throughout Latin America are probably facing a lot of very similar issues, and how deeply this woman's story may be resonating with others here in the room.

Next, we hear a representative of the Mexican organization UNORCA, the National Union of Regional Campesino Organizations, speaking about the damaging effects of free trade on rural areas. The speaker is promoting a very different model of development, based on the idea of food sovereignty. This goes beyond the concept of food security, which means that people have enough food to eat regardless of how or where it was produced. Food sovereignty, on the other hand, means that people have control over their own systems of food production and distribution. Proponents of this model believe that food and agriculture should be exempt from free trade agreements, so that producers can access their own local markets without being forced to compete with foreign agribusiness. They believe this is not only a matter of rural livelihoods, but of overall national security as well.[1]

As a short interlude in the meeting, a group of people who grow medicinal plants in Mexico stand up to perform a song about the strength and beauty and struggles of campesinos. One person strums a guitar as the other two sing, their voices soaring and warbling with such *fuerza* (force). After this, Carlos Marentes (the founder and director of Sin Fronteras) speaks about his work and about the May 1st Day Without Workers, when 70 percent of the daily workers from Juárez just didn't cross the bridge to work in El Paso. He compares U.S. immigration policy to a domestic violence case, in which the husband abuses his wife not to make her leave home, but to keep her there and control her. Despite its anti-immigrant policies, the U.S. depends on the labor of Mexican migrant workers. The approach we really need, Mr. Marentes argues, is to ensure basic human rights to all migrants and to focus on why they're leaving Mexico. It's not a situation that can be addressed only north of the border. "We have two Mexicos," he says. "One is here, in Sonora, Chihuahua, Oaxaca—all of the Mexican Republic. The other Mexico that is struggling is on the other side of the border." He believes both of these areas must be addressed, so that "all Mexicans have a right to live and work and die in the land where they were born."

The conference ends with an exuberant *"Globalizemos la lucha!"* Globalize the struggle! It's the same idea, I realize, that Sister Lolita was talking about yesterday. The hope for small producers is to organize— locally, nationally, and globally. These small rural groups don't have political power individually, but as a coalition, they do. Peasants[2] actually comprise just under 50 percent of the entire global population, so by taking advantage of their numbers and joining together, they can have a stronger voice in decisions about trade and the use of natural resources. Those discussions are usually dominated by political leaders and big businesses, but now a group of "common people" has arrived to claim a seat at the table as well.

Here amid the energy of this gathering, I can't help thinking it's one of the most hopeful, inspiring things I've witnessed thus far on our trip. We're standing at the frontier of something entirely new, a growing movement that could really change the course of things. Thinking back over the past few days and the complex issues we've confronted, I feel that what we are seeing right now is yet another truly tangible source of hope.

La Vía Campesina: The International Peasant Movement

In 1993, forty-six leaders from rural organizations around the world gathered for a conference in Mons, Belgium. Realizing they all faced similar challenges as a result of structural adjustment programs, free trade agreements, and the corporate control of food systems, they decided that the only way to preserve their livelihoods was to join together and establish a stronger voice in discussions over global agriculture and food policy. To this end, they created the Vía Campesina International Peasant Movement and began working to define an alternative model of agriculture in which the production, processing, distribution, and consumption of food would no longer be controlled by a handful of transnational corporations, but by local people and communities.

This vision is best expressed by the term *food sovereignty*, coined by La Vía Campesina in 1996 and further refined by other movements, organizations, and research institutions over the past twelve years. In essence, food sovereignty is the right of people, communities, and nations to define their own agricultural and food policies. It is the right to base those policies on the needs of local producers and consumers, to regulate domestic agriculture in order to achieve sustainable development objectives, and to restrict trade in order to protect growers from foreign competition. While the concept of food sovereignty does not negate trade altogether, it promotes trade practices that are rooted in the pursuit of domestic and local food security, as opposed to solely profit-driven motives. In simple terms, food sovereignty is the right of people to produce their own food on their own land, in ways appropriate for their own environment and culture. Several NGOs and social movements have included the concept of food sovereignty in their policy statements, and it is now also recognized by the United Nations, certain political parties, and an ever-growing number of citizens worldwide.

The members of La Vía Campesina today include over a hundred organizations of small- and medium-scale farmers, landless workers, indigenous communities, and farm laborers from fifty-six counties throughout Asia, Africa, Europe, and North and South America. These members participate in demonstrations and marches against globalization, hold gatherings to share information and formulate their policy positions, spread public awareness in response to human rights violations against farmers, and support one another's struggles for land, credit, water, and political participation. They have also led relief efforts, such as an international fundraising campaign after the 2004 tsunami in Thailand, to distribute resources directly to local community organizations so they could define their own priorities for relief and reconstruction.

Above all, the members of La Vía Campesina have established an international presence and voice for rural people throughout the world, and have claimed a place at the table so that they too may participate in the dialogue over policies that directly affect their lives.

(See reference section for source material.)

That evening, we have some free time to walk around the oldest part of Mexico City, where the *zócalo* (main plaza), *catedral* and ornate colonial buildings rest atop a buried world of ancient stone ruins, the old Aztec capital of Tenochtitlán. The city is humming with life, even at night. In tent-stands lit up as bright as daylight along the sidewalk, people sell CDs, toys, clothes, radios, kitchenware, snacks, all sorts of mass-produced wares; a group practices Aztec drumming and dancing in front of the cathedral; vendors roast sweet corn on little grills along the street; the subways are jam-packed with bodies . . . so much movement and chaotic pulsing energy here in this urban labyrinth.

Fortunately, two men from the conference this afternoon have come along to guide us through the unfamiliar streets, and to share anecdotes about the places we pass. One of them is Camerino Aparicio González, an indigenous activist from the state of Puebla, who is planning to accompany us during the next few days of our journey. As we walk along, Camerino tells me about his work with an organization of Totonaco and Nahuatl subsistence farmers in the mountains of Puebla. To restore the traditional agricultural practices of his people, Camerino says, it is necessary to also restore the ancient religion and philosophy about humans' role on the earth. He believes these things are very connected, and his organization works to reclaim not only indigenous agriculture practices but also indigenous spiritual beliefs. The streets are loud and Camerino speaks very fast, so I only catch about a third of what he's saying, but it's enough to see how very excited he is about this work.

After walking for a few hours, we head over to the Quaker meeting house where we'll be staying for the night. On a side street tucked away from the noise and bustle of the city, we find the old four-story building with its facade of little purple tiles, huge windows, and a sign reading *"Casa de los Amigos: Centro de Paz y Entendimiento Internacional."* House of Friends: Center for Peace and International Understanding.

August 3rd

Meeting with Diputada Susana Monreal Avila, member of the Mexican Congress, to discuss NAFTA and migration

I wake up early the next morning, eager to look around and learn more about the Casa de los Amigos. Originally built as the studio and home of Mexican painter José Clemente Orozco, it has been used for the past fifty years by the Quakers of Mexico City as a religious meeting place, a center for social service programs, temporary lodging for Central American refugees, a venue for cultural events, office space for small nonprofits, and a guest house for activist-oriented students and travelers. It's a large home with sunlit rooms and secluded open-air patios, a colorful dining room with a round table where everyone eats together, two kitchens, a meeting area with big windows and a circle of wooden chairs, and a living room with couches, coffee tables, and lots of bookshelves.

I pick up a copy of *La Voz de la Casa*, a seasonal newsletter written by the Casa staff and volunteers, and page through it with interest. There's a short piece about the house's effort to support small Mexican producers by selling their crafts here, and one section in particular jumps out at me:

They do not need their products to appear in supermarkets around the world; they just need a few promoters, like a small peace center in Mexico City, who respect their products enough to sell them and split the profits. These profits allow the communities to improve their infrastructure, such as schools and health-care facilities, but perhaps more importantly, it allows them to stay in their communities as opposed to migrating north.

Yes, I think. This is exactly what we've been hearing over and over the past few days: the need for domestic markets that support small producers. If residents of Mexico City consumed more goods produced in the campo (rather than mass-produced and imported goods), then rural people might not be migrating by the hundreds of thousands, as they are right now. But are politicians in the U.S.—and proponents of free trade—aware of this possibility?

After breakfast at the Casa, we make our way back out into the city, through a big outdoor market, and onto the crowded subway. I am amused to see a solitary corn plant growing in a little patch of dirt and bushes by the subway station, a reminder of the prevalence and importance of this country's staple crop. We cross a bridge over the busy street and walk to the Mexican congressional building, where we've come to hear one congressperson's perspective on issues of trade and migration. I keep thinking about what that man in Santa Isabel told us a couple days ago: "The Mexican government is not interested in farmers. We need our government [officials] to get out of their offices and understand the countryside." Given his sentiment, I'm looking forward to hearing how a member of Congress will explain the situation.

We wait in front of the Congress building and are soon met by Laura Carlsen, a writer and policy analyst who has lived in Mexico City for over twenty years and currently directs the Americas Policy Program.[3] Laura greets everyone warmly and accompanies us into the building for a meeting with *Diputada Federal*[4] Susana Monreal Avila, a member of the left-wing PRD party and head of the House Agriculture Commission.

We sit at long tables arranged in a U-shape around the meeting room, and Ms. Avila begins with a slide presentation about how NAFTA has affected Mexico. She tells us about her own home state of Zacatecas, where agriculture is the main economic activity, and where there's an exceptionally high rate of out-migration. In fact, more than half of the state's population currently resides in the U.S., sending home almost two million dollars per day to support the elderly, women, and children left behind. (That may sound like a lot of money, but it's actually less than two dollars per day per person living in the state.) "It's hard to say this," Ms. Avila tells us, "but that's how we've been able to survive."

She then goes on to explain how both U.S. and Mexican government policies contribute to this problem. Under the free trade agreement, Mexican crops are subject to competition with cheaper U.S. crops, which receive huge subsidy payments and are therefore sold below the real cost of production. Last February, Ms. Avila traveled to the U.S. to meet with Secretary Yohans from the USDA and to discuss the U.S. Farm Bill, particularly the way its subsidies are making it impossible for Mexican farmers to compete under a free trade system. Apparently, this meeting was unsuccessful.

The U.S. Farm Bill

The Farm Bill is a large piece of legislation passed by Congress every five to seven years, which defines and funds a wide range of government programs, including food stamps and nutrition, agricultural research, animal welfare, forestry, rural electricity and water supply, foreign food aid, and—most importantly here—subsidy payments to commodity crop producers. Because year-to-year fluctuation in crop yields and prices makes farming an inherently risky profession, such payments have historically been used to provide more stability to growers.

However, the design of Farm Bill subsidy programs has changed significantly throughout history. The original program of the 1930s and 1940s paid farmers to idle some of their land and to store grain during years of abundance, to prevent flooding the market and pushing prices too low. The government also purchased grain and held it in national reserves, thereby regulating supply in order to stabilize prices. But beginning in the mid 1960s, this approach of curbing overproduction was replaced by one that instead encouraged maximum production and low prices. Secretary of Agriculture Earl Butz encouraged farmers to plant "fence row to fence row" and to put their entire harvest on the market. Under this new policy, producers were guaranteed a minimum price for their grain, and if market prices dropped below that level, government payments would make up the difference. As corn production increased and prices fell, the government indeed paid billions of dollars to support the surplus production, ensuring that farmers would break even and continue producing corn.

(Without such intervention, the low prices would probably have caused many farmers to switch to other crops.)

This system continued until 1996, when Congress made changes in order to comply with World Trade Organization (WTO) rules for open market competition. Because subsidies constitute an unfair trade advantage, the 1996 Farm Bill called for direct farm payments to be phased out entirely by 2001. This bill also removed the final measures for supply regulation, which until then had still required farmers to idle a portion of their land in order to receive government support. Growers were now allowed to produce as much as possible, under the assumption that new export markets would absorb the surplus production. But this didn't happen, and U.S. grain prices crashed due to oversupply. Commodity groups therefore began lobbying for "emergency payments," and Congress obliged with billions of dollars, which by 2001 accounted for 40 percent of net farm income in twenty-one states (and even higher percentages in others). This newly expanded, record-breaking subsidy program was later locked into place by the 2002 Farm Bill.

Because the new subsidies are based only on acreage rather than current output, the WTO considers them unrelated to production decisions and therefore not "trade-distorting." (A payment that doesn't encourage over-production of a certain crop is assumed not to affect export volumes or prices.) So despite huge payments to corn farmers (at levels ten times the entire Mexican agricultural budget), the U.S. reported "no export subsidy" for corn in 2000 or 2001. But other governments have argued that such payments *do* push world prices downward and therefore violate trade agreements. In 2002, corn exports from the United States were priced at 13 percent below the cost of production (and wheat at 43 percent below), which affected the international market price for these crops.

The main beneficiaries of such policies are large agribusiness corporations such as Cargill and Archer Daniels Midland, which gain access to an abundant supply of artificially cheap grain for making processed foods and animal feed. Because the raw materials are so cheap, these companies are able to sell their final products to the public at competitively low prices, yet still make a profit. (These same two corporations are also the largest corn exporters to Mexico, where they own shares in the major grain companies and tortilla manufacturers that import and process U.S. corn.) Mexican beneficiaries of the U.S. Farm Bill include large food processing companies and livestock farms, which reap higher profits thanks to the availability of cheap U.S. grain.

For small- and medium-scale producers, however, the subsidies received by large U.S. farms create a situation of impossible competition. Many grassroots organizations and research institutes have critiqued the U.S. Farm Bill and recommended new policies that would benefit family farmers in both the U.S. and Mexico. Oxfam recommends a new subsidy program to support small producers engaged in sustainable agriculture, and the Institute for Agriculture and Trade Policy (IATP) has called for a price floor for commodity crops and a "competition title" to improve antitrust enforcement against agribusiness firms. IATP maintains that a reformed U.S. Farm Bill could reduce migration by improving the bleak conditions of rural areas in both Mexico and the United States.

(See reference section for source material.)

Right now, Ms. Avila explains, Mexico is still permitted to use some trade barriers to reduce foreign competition, but those will end completely when NAFTA enters its final stage in January 2008. She reminds us that many Mexican producers still farm on tiny plots with mules and horse-drawn plows, and that such farms will be in direct competition with large, mechanized U.S. farms that produce more grain per hectare at a lower price.

In light of this situation, Ms. Avila believes the Mexican government should provide more support to its corn and bean producers so they can compete in the market. But she says there is too much opposition from the more conservative factions of the government. The House of Deputies has actually written and passed its own Farm Bill outlining a program of increased support for Mexican growers, but this hasn't been able to pass through the more conservative Senate. And although Ms. Avila's own party, the PRD, is a significant political force in the nation, it becomes a minority when the conservative Partido Acción Nacional (PAN) and formerly ruling Partido Revolucionario Institucional (PRI) form an alliance. So bills to support small farmers get stuck, while others for commercial agriculture and foreign interests are passed. The PRD has strong positions, Ms. Avila says, but it's very hard to advance them given this situation.

With such a large number of small farmers and low-income urban laborers in this country, I wonder, *why haven't those groups been able to obtain more*

political representation of their often overlapping viewpoints and policy inter-
ests, or forged their own political party capable of attracting the majority vote
in Congress? Do most democratic governments truly act on behalf of the
majority of their citizens? Or is the political party system here in Mexico part
*of the **problem** more than the solution? I feel frustrated, knowing the inner*
workings of Mexican politics are far too complex and unfamiliar for me to
understand or evaluate at this moment.

NAFTA is currently being discussed extensively in the House, Ms. Avila
tells us, and the vast majority of representatives want to reopen the agriculture chapter for further negotiation. "Mexico signed a treaty with
the most powerful agricultural exporters in the world, under unequal
conditions," she asserts. "A treaty for equals, signed by those who are
unequal, is unjust and should not be ratified."

In her view, free trade has only worsened inequalities between the
two countries—economically, socially, environmentally, and in terms
of food security—and that has contributed to increased migration. "The
people of the countryside do not want to leave," she tells us firmly.
"They want to stay in their homes, on their land, with their families.
But lacking the means to feed their children or to repay the debts generated by their farms, they are forced to leave for the U.S."

*Isn't it oversimplified, I think to myself, to say that **everybody** in the campo*
wants to stay in Mexico? Many young people who have grown up watching
television and hearing stories from the U.S. are probably itching to leave their
villages and cross the border in search of adventure or fortune or social status,
whatever idealistic dreams they carry, but I wonder how many of those people
would return home again after a few years if there were actually viable ways
to make a living here. I wonder what percentage of current migrants would
still choose to live in the U.S. if the economic situation here in the Mexican
countryside were different. . . . But unless things change dramatically, how
will we ever know?

Ms. Avila tells us there's an article in the Mexican Constitution allowing the government to reopen and modify treaties that conflict with
federal law, but that the U.S. and Canadian governments are both
opposed to renegotiation of NAFTA. Some politicians have apparently
threatened to reopen *other* parts of the treaty (which could be to the dis-
advantage of Mexico) if the agriculture chapter were reopened.

NAFTA: Effects on Agriculture

NAFTA required the immediate removal of all non-tariff barriers for agricultural goods, and a gradual fifteen-year phase-out of tariffs for crops such as corn, beans, and milk. However, the Mexican government eliminated tariffs much sooner than required, and agricultural trade—particularly exports of U.S. grain and Mexican fruits and vegetables—grew very rapidly. The USDA Foreign Agriculture Service describes this as "one of the most successful trade agreements in history," asserting that increased trade and investment have benefited both farmers and consumers in all three countries. Yet opponents maintain that NAFTA has only benefited a few large-scale growers and food processing corporations, while devastating smaller producers. In Mexico, small farmers (who still comprised 25 percent of the population prior to NAFTA) had historically grown corn as a staple for home consumption as well as for the domestic market, supplying up to a quarter of total national production in some years. But as imports of cheaper U.S. corn entered the market, these farmers could no longer find a buyer for their crops.

The architects of NAFTA predicted that cheap imports and declining corn prices would simply prompt farmers to switch to other crops such as fruits and vegetables, in which Mexico has a comparative advantage over the U.S. (due to its cheap labor force and winter growing season). But this change did not take place to the extent predicted, because only large landholders in the north—located on flat, fertile, irrigated land with access to credit, technology, and established marketing channels—were able to make such a shift. These farms are typically contracted out by U.S. produce companies, which prefer to deal with large commercial growers rather than peasant farmers. Meanwhile, the vast majority of producers live in central and southern Mexico, on small plots that are generally unsuitable for horticulture due to steep slopes, poor soil, and irregular rainfall. These farmers are also unable to afford the high initial start-up costs of shifting to agroexport production, and are therefore excluded from the new export market. In addition, those who assumed that farmers would readily shift away from basic grain failed to consider the dietary and cultural significance of corn in rural Mexico. As a result, only a few large-scale growers have gained access to U.S. markets, and their success masks the plight of small farmers throughout the country, just as higher overall GDP can mask the declining incomes of the poor.

Throughout the course of NAFTA, rural Mexico has faced ever-increasing poverty, environmental degradation, social unrest, and out-migration. Over two million farmers have fled the countryside, and each year hundreds of thousands more risk their lives to cross the border in search of work. Rather than profiting from new markets, these displaced farmers have instead become the *labor force* for large agroexport farms, picking tomatoes and peppers for U.S. markets under some of the worst living and working conditions in Mexico. While their incomes may have increased (contributing to higher overall GDP), these workers also face declining nutrition, separation from their families, job instability, and higher living costs due to the loss of self-provisioning.

Yet advocates of NAFTA point to Mexico's increased GDP as an indicator of success, arguing that poverty and uneven distribution of wealth are the failure of domestic policies rather than free trade. Opponents reply that NAFTA has prevented the governments from enacting better policies, and has increased corporate influence over national politics. Many also point out that the impacts of NAFTA have been unevenly distributed among member nations, as the U.S. imports mainly nonessential products like coffee and fruit, while Mexico imports vast quantities of basic staple foods. Such trade has a greater impact on food security in Mexico, where a large percentage of the population is involved in agriculture and depends upon corn for both income and daily sustenance.

The debate over NAFTA is part of a broader debate about free trade in general. Proponents view trade as a solution to poverty and underdevelopment, with each country exporting goods for which it has a comparative advantage, and using the revenue to import other goods. But opponents argue that the reality on the ground is very different from this idealized economic model, and that free trade in agriculture reduces food security, destroys rural livelihoods, and consolidates wealth in the hands of the few. (During the time of NAFTA, for example, falling corn prices and rising tortilla prices have hurt both producers and consumers, while large processing companies have reaped greater profits.)

(See reference section for source material.)

When the presentation ends, everyone has questions.

"What *is* Mexico doing to support its farmers?" Annette wants to know. "And what can we do in the U.S. to support you?

"The federal government does have some programs for farmers, but they have raised the requirements and really restricted access to them," she replies.

I think back to the program Rogelio described, in which the government provides 60 percent of funds if a farmer can provide the other 40 percent, which is impossible for small farmers to do without working for many years in the U.S. to save up the money. I wonder to myself, *Is this the type of program Ms. Avila is talking about?*

In response to Annette's second question, she replies, "What you're doing right now is essential. Please spread the word in the U.S. that we signed a treaty as though we were economic equals, and that it's first affecting Mexico but will wind up affecting the U.S. too."

"Are there any parts of NAFTA that are beneficial to Mexico?" Rachel asks.

"Yes, some parts may be considered beneficial," Ms. Avila replies, "but they do not help farmers or the population as a whole."

She explains how President Felipe Calderón applauds NAFTA based on increased exports and a higher GDP, but how such benefits have only been enjoyed by an elite few, such as the owners of large companies and agribusiness firms. Several of the world's richest billionaires live here in Mexico, while at the same time, about 50 percent of the population lives in poverty or extreme poverty, without an adequate and secure food supply. In a country of such vast inequality, do measures of overall production and income really mean anything? Do they signify progress? According to this representative, only a wealthy minority has benefited from NAFTA, while the majority of the population bears the costs.

"If NAFTA can't be changed, what options remain?" wonders Jan.

"That's what we're trying to figure out," she replies. "But we [the House] don't have as much power as the president and Senate, and we'll need to work together as a whole government if we are to effectively help people in the countryside."

"If you could rewrite Mexican agricultural policy yourself, what would you change?" Denise asks.

Ms. Avila's answer is quick and to the point. "Protect corn and bean production as a national strategy, as the basis of our food sovereignty and our culture."

She then gives the floor to Dr. Hector Orlanga from the Center for Rural Studies, a national research organization that provides information to members of Congress to inform their policy decisions. Dr. Orlanga wants to provide more background to help us understand the situation of Mexico's campesinos.

The average corn grower in the U.S. has ninety hectares and can produce eight or nine tons per hectare, he says, while the average grower in Mexico has only three hectares and can produce about two tons per hectare. This is because U.S. corn production is mostly on flat, fertile, irrigated land, with high-tech equipment and an abundance of chemical inputs, requiring less than one hour of labor to produce each ton of corn. In Mexico, on the other hand, the vast majority of production is on marginal, sloped, nonirrigated land, requiring many days of labor to produce each ton.[5] Even if NAFTA were renegotiated, Dr. Orlanga says, the Mexican government would still need to devote more resources to the countryside in order to improve production.

But he does mention one program that's been quite successful. It's called the *Tres por Uno*, Three for One, in which the municipal, state, and federal governments each give a dollar for every dollar sent home by migrants (for those who are registered in the program). This allows people in rural Mexico to start projects such as putting up a greenhouse, digging a well, or investing in a herd of animals, so that those remaining in the villages can support themselves rather than having to migrate as well. Many workers in the U.S. have formed what are called "hometown associations," which are like clubs that jointly send money back to their hometowns in Mexico, in order to start viable enterprises that will support those workers when they return home. Sixty percent of the Three for One budget currently goes to Zacatecas, where people have become very well organized in order to take advantage of it. But if *everyone* started signing up, Dr. Orlanga notes, there wouldn't be enough money in the program's budget.[6]

To me, the success of this program is yet another indication that people are creative in finding ways to survive, and often need support just to get started. They're not asking for handouts or indefinite aid from the government, just for an initial investment to create something that will become self-sustaining in the long run. And they're also asking for government policies that allow those small enterprises to survive, by protecting them from unfair competition. That's all people need—not an ongoing welfare system, just an initial boost and then some basic protections. But do most politicians or citizens outside the campo see it this way?

"How does the middle class here view NAFTA?" someone asks. "Since they're not the ones being hurt the most or benefiting the most?"

"The middle class suffers from much political apathy," Ms. Avila replies. "They feel it's not their problem, and they don't get involved."

"What is your overall vision for the Mexican countryside?" Brian wants to know. "To mechanize and become like the U.S., with only 2 percent of the population still on the land farming, or to retain a certain percentage of people in the campo?"

"Our priority is the farmers," she says. "That the food in this country is produced by Mexican farmers, and that we value them as first class citizens. That we conserve our food sovereignty, and produce food for Mexico before even thinking about exporting."

*Although I appreciate this viewpoint, I don't feel that Brian's question has been fully answered. I'd still like to know how she defines agricultural development, and whether she'd like to see farming become more mechanized, with fewer people in rural areas. When she speaks of the U.S. advantages in production, comparing them to the mule-drawn plows still used in many parts of Mexico, I wonder if she considers all traditional agricultural practices to be underdeveloped and backward, and if she envisions large machinery and irrigation projects and more chemical inputs. Or does she want to protect Mexican farmers from foreign competition so they **can** retain certain traditional techniques, in addition to moving toward newer methods of low-input (and in fact, highly productive) sustainable agriculture? Does the proposed farm bill that she mentioned just imitate the U.S. bill, subsidizing large, mechanized, high-input and heavily polluting operations, or is it something entirely different? I'm puzzled by her response, and wish she had shared her ultimate vision for Mexican agriculture.*

"What's the stance of the PRD on removing agriculture from free trade agreements altogether?" Martha asks.

As far as I can tell, she doesn't answer that one directly either, but just repeats that the PRD has very strong positions that are hard to advance given the current political situation. I'm disappointed that we couldn't spend more time here and move beyond what struck me as sound bites to a more in-depth discussion of these issues . . . but our time for the meeting is over, and Ms. Avila makes her way around the table shaking the hand of each person individually, thanking us for coming, and exchanging the customary light kiss on the cheek. Eric later says that politicians like her are very rare.

Before leaving the room, I take a few minutes to scribble the following reflections in my notebook:

*I'm glad we were able to talk with a congressperson who is so concerned with the plight of farmers, to see that such a perspective actually **does** exist within*

*the government, even though it lacks the majority vote needed to affect poli-
cies. I really wonder if the farmers we met in Santa Isabel and Anáhuac are
aware that such support for them exists in Congress, and what they would
have said at this meeting. But at the same time, I'm also curious what a congressperson from the conservative PAN party would have told us. . . I would
have liked to hear those arguments as well, to engage in a dialogue with someone from a different perspective. In fact, I wish we could have relayed some of
the farmers' comments to a **pro**-NAFTA politician and listened to his/her
response. Wouldn't that be more productive than continuing to talk with people who reinforce similar ideas and perspectives that we all seem to share? I
wonder if it would have been possible to arrange such a meeting, whether a
politician in support of free trade would have been willing to talk with us.
And I wonder what might happen if people had interactions like this more
often, listening to opposing viewpoints rather than echoing the same ones
back and forth to each other. I hope that when I return home after this trip, I
will be able to share my thoughts and experiences with a wide audience, both
people who are familiar with these perspectives and those who are not, people
who readily agree and those who have counterarguments to challenge my own.*

In the lobby of the Congress building, we admire a huge woodcut
depicting the history of Mexico—highlighting corn as the basis of the
economy, honoring the pre-Hispanic people, showing peasants marching for land reform in the 1920s—and I wonder how the history we're
creating right now would appear on this woodcut. What symbols would
be used to represent the massive exodus of young people from this
country?

We gather back on the sidewalk for a few minutes to talk with Laura
Carlsen, who wants to fill us in on a few more things. When Vicente
Fox was president, she says, he actually sent a letter to President Bush
asking to renegotiate NAFTA, but then acquiesced when the U.S. government refused. But small family farmers in the U.S. and Canada *also*
want renegotiation, Laura says, and it's remarkable how much com-
monality exists between small-scale producers in all three countries.

I think back over the criticisms of NAFTA we've been hearing the
last few days, and the fact that nobody has framed it as "U.S. profiting at the expense of Mexico" or "north profiting at the expense of
south." Instead, they've been talking about "big business profiting
at the expense of small producers." If you fall into this latter group
of small producers, the breakdown of government protection and
regional/domestic markets is a threat to your livelihood, no matter
where you live.

Laura says people are trying to predict what will happen in 2008 when NAFTA goes into full effect, but that it's hard to say. Much of the impact has already been felt, she says, because imports into Mexico have been violating the agreement and exceeding quotas for quite some time. So there might not be any huge change.

Proponents of free trade claim that NAFTA has been successful because the flow of money and goods has increased, but Laura says they're forgetting an important question: What's the relationship between trade and the well-being of the population in general? Should we simply assume that one implies the other? Should we rely on economic theories that say it works that way, or should we actually look on the ground and *see* whether trade is benefiting the common citizen? To me, it seems obvious that we must do the latter . . . but perhaps not everybody wants to look.

Tlaxcala

4

Later that day, we head east into the mountains of Tlaxcala, the smallest state in Mexico and a region heavily impacted by migration. I fall asleep on the bus, wakening after we've left the city and are rolling through pine-forested hills in the countryside, beneath those dark-purple rain clouds that come every afternoon. We pass several small towns, tucked into valleys surrounded by cornfields and pastures of grazing animals. Practically everywhere you look, there is corn—in fields beside houses, in rectangular clearings among the trees, corn tucked into every nook and cranny of the landscape. Even when we pass through larger towns, I see it growing in backyards, in vacant lots between buildings, in little patches of land beside the highway. . . . *Sin maíz, no hay país,* they say. Without corn, there is no country. The truth of that phrase is impossible to miss here, as though the land is chanting it over and over, with every field.

We soon arrive at the bus depot in San Martín Texmelucan, a city situated on a vast plateau way up in the mountains, and switch into a smaller local bus that's more like a van. Winding our way along a narrow road farther into the campo, Eric gives some background on the region and his own connection here. These hills were originally all covered in trees, he says, but after the conquest, Spain promptly cut down Tlaxcala's forests to build its famous *armada*. With no roots to hold the fragile topsoil in place, and with the introduction of the plow and sheep grazing by the Spaniards, soil began washing down the slopes in heavy rains. By the 1930s, Tlaxcala (one of Mexico's most powerful city-states during precolonial times) had become the country's most heavily eroded region, and its poorest.

Colonization also brought the *encomienda* system, in which Spanish colonists and bureaucrats were granted control over large tracts of land and all the human inhabitants, under an agreement to make the land "productive" and give a portion of this wealth to the Spanish crown. So indigenous people were bound in quasi-slavery, laboring in the fields and mines of the encomiendas to extract natural resources for Spain.

The encomienda gradually gave way to the *hacienda* system, in which people were allotted small plots of land to grow their own food, but were still required to provide labor and taxes to the landowners. This continued even after independence from Spain, with native people working as peons on land that remained in the hands of a small wealthy elite of European descent.

Listening to this impromptu history lesson, I muse about our tendency to blame NAFTA for issues in the Mexican countryside. Clearly it does play a large role, but I think it's important to remember the historical context as well, the backdrop against which these recently added factors are playing out. Thinking about colonization, I realize that the campesinos of Tlaxcala were already in a very compromised position, long before free trade agreements entered the stage.

But in the 1930s, Eric continues, after the peasant uprising and Mexican Revolution, President Lázaro Cárdenas initiated major land reform, confiscating land from the elite and distributing it back to peasants under the ejido system. After nearly four hundred years of domination, indigenous people finally had the right to collectively manage and control their own land.

As Eric describes it, many landless peasants were roaming the countryside in search of a newly designated ejido, and would descend upon a place in hopes of settling there. So the villages here in Tlaxcala are not ancient communities that have been in place for centuries, like in other parts of Mexico. These have really only existed for about seventy years, and were established by people from various cultural and geographic backgrounds.

So, I think to myself, *they can't just return to traditional farming methods, as many people presume the term "sustainable agriculture" to mean . . . because people in this particular area of Tlaxcala do not* **have** *a long tradition of farming the land where they now live. Colonialism was like a big broom that swept through and drastically altered the landscape, moved people around, interrupted the passing of traditional knowledge . . . basically scrambled the playing board, mixed up the pieces, and changed a lot of the rules. Not the type of situation where you can just pick up like nothing happened, way back where your great-grandparents left off!*

People soon began farming the new ejidos, and overall food production throughout the countryside increased. Then, in the 1970s, another major change impacted peasant farmers in central and southern Mexico—the Green Revolution. Extension agents from the international crop research center in Puebla began to travel throughout this region, giving farmers "technological packages" of hybrid seed and chemicals to try in their fields. At first, yields increased and the new technology seemed a success. People began taking out loans to buy more seed and fertilizer, hoping to sell their crop for enough money to repay those loans and earn a profit. Encouraged by extension agents to grow as much of the new high-yielding corn as possible, they abandoned traditional systems of intercropping and began planting entire fields of corn to sell in the market. With the Green Revolution, people basically shifted from producing the majority of their own food, to producing for the market and using money to buy food and other basic needs.

Although this worked initially, farmers soon began noticing that it took more fertilizer each year to maintain the same high yields. Erosion and the use of synthetic fertilizer led to a net loss of organic matter from the fields each year and, hence, a decline of the soil's natural fertility. So farmers began taking out larger loans to buy even more fertilizer, becoming trapped on a sort of treadmill in which they needed the expensive inputs in order to grow enough corn to pay back their debts. By the 1970s, farmers' production costs in Tlaxcala were increasing each year, while their yields were steadily decreasing.

Campesino a Campesino training center in the village of Vicente Guerrero, and local fields where sustainable agriculture practices are being implemented to increase soil fertility and crop yields

This is the situation Eric found when he arrived in the village of Vicente Guerrero, here in Tlaxcala, back in the late 1970s. Much of the land was barren and unproductive, since the topsoil had washed away and

The Green Revolution and Peasant Agriculture

During its first two decades, the Rockefeller-sponsored Mexican Agriculture Program (MAP) focused on commercial production rather than small-scale peasant agriculture, breeding crops for urban consumers and export markets while neglecting the basic staples that sustained the country's rural population. Although national grain production increased from the 1940s to 1960s, this growth occurred almost entirely within the large-scale commercial sector.

By 1960, a few MAP scientists suggested expanding the program to smallholders, who comprised the vast majority of Mexican producers, and the Rockefeller Foundation sent agricultural economist Herrell DeGraff to travel the countryside and investigate the possibility of such a project. DeGraff concluded that subsistence farms should indeed be modernized and shifted to commercial production, but that traditional culture posed a major obstacle to such changes. In response, MAP began to deliberately promote its technologies to peasant farmers.*

Beginning in 1960, however, MAP was gradually absorbed into the creation of CIMMYT, the International Maize and Wheat Improvement Center, which initiated a major attempt (later referred to as the Green Revolution) to extend modern science to traditional agriculture throughout the world. In Mexico, the Puebla Project (begun in 1967) sent extension agents to rural villages to distribute packages of hybrid seeds, chemical fertilizers, and insecticides, as well as programs for crop insurance and credit to help people buy the expensive new inputs. By the early 1970s, thousands of small farmers were participating in the new program.

But while the new hybrid varieties and chemical inputs boosted yields initially, they also caused serious long-term environmental damage and public health impacts in rural areas. In order to produce higher yields, the new varieties required synthetic fertilizer, which degraded the soil and failed to replenish organic matter as traditional methods had done.** Moreover, extensionists instructed farmers to sow entire fields to a single crop, which increased the plants' vulnerability to disease and pests and thus required the use of pesticides. As insects developed resistance to those chemicals and pest outbreaks became more common, productivity began to fall. To compensate for the losses, farmers had to use even more fertilizer and pesticide, which began a cycle of ever-increasing chemical use and higher production costs. This also placed pressure on forests, as people eventually had to abandon depleted fields and clear new areas for agriculture.

A 1979 study of the village of Nealtican, Puebla, describes how farmers there rejected the new seeds and chemicals of the Green Revolution (even after a demonstration showing higher yields), because of serious disadvantages and risks in adopting the new technology. By planting many corn varieties on small, interspersed plots, farmers in Nealtican ensured that a potential failure of one variety or plot would not compromise the entire year's harvest. But if all fields were planted to a single hybrid variety, as program extensionists recommended, a crop failure would be devastating. For these farmers, the diversity of traditional systems was a form of crop insurance, and was preferable to the limited insurance plan offered by the Puebla Project. The new methods would have also increased risk by requiring farmers to buy costly pesticides, since high-yielding varieties were susceptible to earworm infestation, while the highly resistant local varieties experienced so little pest damage that no chemicals were necessary. Community members also rejected hybrid corn because of its disagreeable taste and texture, and because it didn't produce enough stalks and leaves to provide animal feed during winter. ("High yielding" referred only to kernels, not the entire plant! In addition, scientists had compared yields of hybrid corn to those of traditional corn without taking into account the *total* yield of corn, beans, and squash from traditional intercropped fields, making it appear that hybrid corn yielded higher. But when Dr. Javier Trujillo de Arriaga studied maize production in Tlaxcala during the 1980s, in an area where traditional practices had not changed dramatically, he found that in many cases—especially when the soil was more dry—the traditionally cultivated fields outproduced those cultivated using chemicals and planted with a single hybrid crop.)

Unlike the story of Nealtican, however, thousands of farmers throughout Mexico (and the world) quickly adopted the new technologies of the Green Revolution, and the ensuing short-term gains in production came at a steep price of deepening poverty and debt, depletion of natural resources, major declines in rural health and nutrition, and extensive deforestation and erosion throughout the countryside. As yields declined and arable land became more scarce, millions of people were forced to leave their homes and migrate to cities in search of work.

Today, a growing number of scientists advocate an alternative approach called agroecology, which they believe could improve production in the Mexican countryside in a more sustainable way. Based on the principles of ecology, agroecology seeks to create agricultural systems that use and reuse locally available resources instead of relying on outside chemical inputs. Unlike the methods and techniques of the Green Revolution, agro-ecological farming is compatible with local environment and culture, founded on indigenous knowledge, and is economically affordable, low risk, and designed to enhance total farm productivity and stability over the long term. This approach is currently being used to intensify production and successfully raise yields in many places throughout the world, and, according to agroecologist Miguel Altieri, it has the potential to raise cereal yields in developing countries by 50 to 200 percent. Moreover, a 1989 report from the National Academy of Sciences announced that successful alternative farms are generally profitable with little financial support from the government, because the costs of production tend to be lower and the production levels more consistent. But to take root and become wide-spread, such alternative models of agriculture will require the same favorable policies, investment, and research that were granted to the architects of the Green Revolution.

---

*Several scientists within the program actually advised against this idea, arguing that rural poverty stemmed from social and economic causes rather than inadequate agricultural techniques, and that the new program could harm millions of subsistence producers. But the Rockefeller Foundation ignored this advice and continued to pursue a narrow approach of increasing production through modern farming techniques.

**In 1975, a few Puebla Project directors privately acknowledged the superiority of traditional fertilizers such as legumes and animal manure, but their commitments to the national fertilizer company and various banks prevented them from actually recommending such methods.

(See reference section for source material.)

exposed an underlying layer of brick-hard subsoil that was impossible to cultivate. Moreover, the original ejidatarios had divided land among their sons, resulting in parcels of only half a hectare to five hectares. So the seventy families of the ejido were struggling to make a living on these small plots of eroded and drought-ridden land, and many people were in debt and unable to produce enough food to support their families. If a crop failed, the men would just travel to Mexico City and work as day laborers (usually in masonry or on the railroad) for the rest of the year. Nearly every able-bodied man in Vicente Guerrero had gone to work in the city at some point.

Around this time, the Mexican Friends Service Committee[1] was organizing summer work camps in rural Tlaxcala, where university students would live for a couple of months and help with various development projects in the communities. One year, volunteers in the village of Vicente Guerrero did a survey to better understand the needs of the community, and found that people's greatest need was to produce enough food to feed their families. So the village and the Mexican Friends Service Committee set up a program for a pair of longer-term volunteers to come and work on a food-security project.

Eric and his partner had been traveling through Mexico at this time, and they stopped overnight at the Casa de los Amigos, where they happened to hear about this volunteer opportunity. They applied to the program and were accepted, which is how Eric came to live in the village of Vicente Guerrero for about three years.

This road was all dirt and potholes back then, he says, and it took hours to reach San Martín. But many things have changed now, due to remittance money sent home from the United States. This is actually a very new phenomenon in the area, Eric explains. Back when he lived here, nobody from Vicente Guerrero had ever been to the United States. Only since 2001 has anyone from the village crossed the border in search of work; today, about half the community's working-age people are in the U.S.

I wonder if it's similar to the stories I've read in Ruben Martínez' book Crossing Over, *which describes migration from a small town in the nearby state of Michoacán. The people there actually do have opportunities for local employment at sawmills and several large farms, but they can get paid twenty times more for similar jobs in the U.S. For a young man to take such a job in Michoacán would be a disgrace and a blow to his pride. The author describes how, after working in the U.S. and earning higher wages, renting an apartment with hot water and an electric stove, and having a small taste of the social mobility that's impossible here, people who have made the journey once are compelled to go back rather than taking poorly paying jobs at home. So it's an oversimplification to say that everyone leaves for lack of job opportunities. . . . I'm aware that the situation is more complicated, in Michoacán and probably here in Tlaxcala as well.*

As Eric talks, I gaze out the window at a rolling landscape of green slopes and valleys, with plots of corn and beans and squash everywhere— sometimes growing in separate fields and sometimes all together, the corn widely spaced amid a sprawling carpet of squash leaves, with viney tendrils of young bean plants curling up the stalks. Some of the corn-fields are also interspersed with rows of agave, prickly pear cactus, and small fruit trees. We pass a couple of villages, each with its own church and little cemetery of winding paths and old white headstones and colorful adornments . . . quaintly picturesque to an outsider like myself.

Much of the land we pass is terraced, bright green stair-steps on the hillsides, and Eric tells how the first terraces in this area were created by government programs in the '70s. The government brought in bulldozers and made terraces that were too straight and didn't follow the natural contours of the land, so they wound up causing even more erosion. Since then, a lot of farmer-led development projects have focused on rebuilding those poorly designed terraces, planting vegetation to hold them in place and adding organic matter to gradually replace the topsoil that was lost. Eric comments that most of the terraces we're passing are quite new, that only a fraction of these existed when he lived here.

The goal of Eric's volunteer project in Vicente Guerrero was to address the issue of low yields and food insecurity by introducing what were considered to be appropriate technology practices such as composting, small-animal husbandry, solar energy, organic gardening, and reforestation. He and his partner were given a small plot in the village to demonstrate these practices. But after two years of work, most of their suggestions had been ignored, and the project seemed a failure in terms of agricultural development. Even though yields in the area were low and continuing to fall, people depended on those meager harvests and were unwilling to risk their entire livelihood by trying new techniques. Eric felt discouraged. Then, near the end of the project, a group of indigenous farmers from Guatemala came to the village to give a four-day workshop on soil and water conservation. Only two people attended, but it was the catalyst for a series of events that greatly impacted the village and surrounding area. That first farmer-to-farmer workshop basically marked the beginning of a new method of agricultural development here in Tlaxcala, not one driven by outside experts or naive volunteers, but by the farmers themselves. It began with just a few people in Vicente Guerrero, but gradually spread and brought many changes to agriculture in this region. We have come to learn about those changes, to see how people have rebuilt the soil and improved their livelihoods during the past thirty years.[2]

I am so intrigued to hear the rest of this story, to examine those terraces up close and learn from the people who cultivate them, to receive answers to all the myriad questions streaming through my head right now. Everything is so new and so fascinating, and I feel like an open vessel, acutely tuned and ready to catch every drop of this experience.

After driving for about half an hour, the bus pulls over to the side of the road near a grove of trees and a school building, and we climb out. This is our stop, Vicente Guerrero.

As the bus moves away down the road, we're left standing in a glorious, tranquil stillness that it seems I haven't felt in ages, after the crowded and smoggy bustle of Mexico City. I inhale deeply and the air smells crisp, of soil and woodsmoke and rain. The earth by the side of the road is a deep reddish-brown, and everything everywhere is *green* . . . the valleys and hills ahead of us wearing a hundred layered cloaks of green.

We head down a steep road adorned with tissue paper decorations and recently paved in orange brick (thanks to remittance money, Eric says). The dirt roads branching off this one are smaller and lined with old adobe walls and houses, unfinished second-story additions of cement and rebar jutting up into the sky, tiny shops adjoining houses, wandering dogs, fenced yards of geese and chickens, grassy plots with grazing mules and burros. Looking around, I am struck by the contrast of adobe brick and farm animals against satellite dishes and large pickup trucks, a juxtaposition that is probably becoming more common as remittance money flows into rural Mexico. I've read stories about entire families working in U.S. factories or meat-processing plants for decades, saving money and returning occasionally to further the construction of a new home, to which they will someday return and live out their old age. Based on the number of large, half-finished, vacant-looking houses we pass, I imagine that's what's happening here.

Some people come to doorsteps and call out, and Eric pauses to hug and heartily greet old acquaintances. As we walk through the streets, he points out the first school garden planted back in the 1970s, a court where he used to play basketball, a park and health center built entirely by community members, the little brick house where Eric and his partner used to live, and the entire street that was once their demonstration farm.

Just down the road from Eric's old house is the Campesino a Campesino training center, a large adobe building with a corrugated tin roof and a colorful mural painted on the outside. We hang out by the road for several minutes, waiting for our hosts to arrive, everyone talking and laughing and taking photos and asking questions. There's an excitement in the air, and it feels as though we've all suddenly come alive, as though a new energy has sprung up since we left the city and arrived out here.

We are soon welcomed into the homey-feeling Campesino a Campe-

The demonstration yard of El Grupo Vicente Guerrero's campesino a campesino training center in Tlaxcala includes a temescal and, behind it, the traditional cone-shaped cuexcomatl for storing maize seeds.

sino center, which has a meeting/dining room with long tables and benches, and an adjoining dormitory with adobe walls, quilt-covered beds, and two bright, airy lofts. We all find places to put our things down in the dormitory and then head back outside, where people are gathering around a huge kiln-shaped structure in the middle of the yard. Smoke wafts from the crackling fire in a small tunnel to one side.

"What's cooking?" someone asks.

"You didn't know we were on the menu, did you?" Eric says with a smile.

It turns out this structure is a *temescal*, an ancient sauna used by indigenous cultures in the highlands of southern Mexico and Guatemala for cleansing and healing purposes. We really *are* invited to "cook" in the oven tonight, or more accurately, to participate in a ritual purification steambath.

Beside the temescal is a giant, funnel-shaped earthen structure with a thatched roof and tiny opening near the ground. It's called a *cuexcomatl* and is used for storing maize seeds to plant the following year. Like the temescal, this ancient custom, which had fallen out of use in modern times, is now being recovered and promoted at farmer-led training centers like this one.

At the other end of the yard is a small kitchen, where two women cook dinner and another prepares bundles of herbs for the temescal ceremony. She pauses to show us the various plants she is using and explains their healing properties. These herbs have been used here for centuries in order to help relax the muscles, draw out infection, and cure sickness. I am excited by the opportunity to participate in such a time-tested healing tradition.

For now, we all gather inside the dining room with our hosts for a short welcome. We first go around the circle introducing ourselves and describing what we hope to gain from this visit. There's Adrian, president of the campesino-led development group here in Vicente Guerrero; Emiliano, a local farmer who wants to share what he's learned and hopes that it will be useful to us; Rogelio, who worked with Eric back in the 1970s and whose father was one of the founders of this ejido; Clara, who smiles warmly and simply says she hopes for a good campesino a campesino exchange. Several other community members and farmers introduce themselves as well, and the meeting begins.

Adrian first gives a brief history of what's happened here in Vicente Guerrero since the late '70s. Following that original workshop with the indigenous Guatemalans, the village assembly decided that Eric and some farmers from the community should travel to Guatemala and learn more about soil and water conservation from the farmers there, then return home and teach everyone what they'd learned. "But we're like St. Thomas," Adrian says with a smile. "We must *see* to believe." So upon their return, the farmers decided to put their new knowledge into practice and teach by example. They began trying out different techniques on small experimental plots, finding the ones that worked best and then applying them to entire fields. At first, people in the village were skeptical. But they eventually began to notice the improvements in those fields and became more willing to experiment themselves.

"Before all this, we were producing less than one ton of corn per hectare," Adrian says. 'With big families, that's not enough to feed everyone for a whole year. It has been a long and difficult process, but we now average three to four tons per hectare, sometimes as much as six."

As the success of these new practices grew, local farmers began holding workshops for other people in the region. They shared their discoveries and encouraged others to start experimenting on a small scale on their own land. "We have always tried to use language that is understandable by other campesinos—education that is horizontal rather than vertical—and that's why we've been successful," Adrian explains. "I don't want to criticize the scientific or academic world, but they use a lot of technical language that people in the campo don't understand."

He says it's taken time to gain acceptance from academia, which originally criticized this movement and failed to recognize it as an effective form of agricultural development. But now that's beginning to change. "We are very happy you're here, to hear about our work and challenges and vision for the future," Adrian concludes.

But for now . . . it's time for the temescal!

We change into bathing suits and gather outside on the lawn. I've never done anything like this and am a little nervous, but also determined not to miss any part of the experience here . . . so, fluttery stomached with anticipation, I join in.

Night has fallen and it's slightly chilly outside, the grass damp on my bare feet. A local man who's leading the ceremony talks briefly about its history and purpose, explaining how entering the temescal represents a return into the womb, and leaving it a rebirth. We'll first be coated in incense, then crawl backwards through the small opening and find a space to sit against the wall.

I enter last, taking a spot beside the doorway, which someone outside covers with a board. Inside the temescal it's completely dark, echoey, and comfortingly, lullingly warm. . . . The air is filled with a smoky aroma and the quiet shifting and breathing of people around the circle. The man leading the ceremony speaks through the darkness about the healing nature of this ritual, both physically and spiritually, and the power to leave behind anything we may want to shed when we reenter the world. Then he slowly pours a little water onto the hot stones in front of the tunnel where the fire was. The water sizzles and steams a bit, and a wave of warmer air moves across the room. We sit in silence in the pitch black, smoky dark. I lean against the cool wall of the temescal and breathe in, then out, slowly, reminding myself that this is a safe space, a cocoon. I imagine the whole planet, and on it the land we call México, and in the southern mountains the village of Vicente Guerrero, and in one little yard, this warm dome-shaped cocoon with all of us gathered together inside. Right now. Here. This moment.

The leader passes around a plate of aloe vera leaves, which we split in half to rub the watery gel over our skin. We also pass around bundles of herbs, to slap against parts of our bodies that may be stiff or sore. For a long time, it is quiet, no sound except breathing and the slapping of leaves on skin. Occasionally someone speaks, in Spanish or English, telling what they'd like to leave behind. Fear, prejudgments, doubt, all those things that hinder effective activism and engagement in the world. The temperature gradually climbs, and we sing a chant that echoes and reverberates loudly in this round chamber. *La tierra es mi cuerpo, el agua es mi sangre, el aire es mi aliento, el fuego es mi espíritu* (The earth is my body, the water is my blood, the air is my breath, the fire is my spirit).

When we finally leave the temescal to calls of "happy birth" from everyone inside, someone outside the door pours cold water all over each of us to close our pores back up. It's a jolting shock to the skin, but also fantastically invigorating.

Once dry and clothed, feeling refreshed, renewed, and (for some of us) a bit giddy, we gather in the dining room for a late meal. It's our first truly home-cooked food of the journey, and is by far the very best we've eaten yet. There are warm, freshly made tortillas wrapped in a cloth, juicy papaya, a salad of tomatoes and sliced cucumber (grown in this village), lemon verbena tea, a thick spiced apple sauce, and green beans cooked with *requesón*, a homemade sort of sweet cottage cheese. Especially after our long day and experience in the temescal, this meal feels like the most comforting and deeply nourishing thing in the world. We talk and laugh around the table, enjoying this delicious food and each other's company . . . and I feel unspeakably joyful to be here in the village of Vicente Guerrero in this wonderful place tonight.

August 4th

I wake next morning to the sound of birds, barking dogs, voices, a radio playing in the distance, someone passing by on the road calling announcements through a megaphone, the smell of grass and woodsmoke and cooking food. *Probably the typical backdrop to a morning in Vicente Guerrero*, I think to myself. Looking out the loft window, over a hillside of winding dirt roads and scattered rooftops with their identical juglike water tanks, I am so full of curiosity about life here, about the seventy or so families for whom this place is home, and what their lives are like. But I realize that no matter how long I were to stay here in Vicente Guerrero, I would probably remain a stranger to some degree and would never fully know.

That's just the way it is, I think, *and another reason why farmer-to-farmer development is more effective than projects run by outsiders. How could we possibly know what is best, in a place so foreign to us?*

We gather for breakfast and enjoy a delicious meal of fresh tortillas, pinto beans, cooked broccoli with melted homemade cheese, slices of papaya, and *atole*, a thick creamy hot chocolate made with cornmeal. I breathe in the aromas and savor every bit of this incredible food.

After breakfast, one of the women in the kitchen teaches Rachel and Annette how to make tortillas, and I watch them roll out the dough and lay it carefully on the stovetop. It amazes me to think how many diverse ways people have found, all over the world, to make seeds into bread!

We soon gather again in the dining room for a more detailed presentation about the rural development group here in Vicente Guerrero and the broader Campesino a Campesino Movement of which it is part.

"This is an extraordinary village," Eric begins by telling us, "because they work very hard but have been willing to try new things." In the U.S., he explains, we are used to innovation as a constant reality, so it's hard for us to understand how significant that is here. To experiment with new practices is to risk being ridiculed by your neighbors, to risk your family's security and your whole livelihood. That takes a lot of courage. "Some of the people in this room are the pioneers who started this movement and have been very influential in it . . . and some of them, by now, are world travelers to a greater degree than many of you," Eric says. "For me, it's a real privilege to have you come to this village and meet the people who trained me, who set me on my course for thirty years."

Next, people around the room introduce themselves: Vicente Pelcastre, Roque Sánchez, and "El Padrino" (thus nicknamed because he has so many godchildren), three of the men who worked with Eric thirty years ago. There's Anastacio Sarmiento Sánchez, the current president of this town, who says he started working with Eric and the others when he was only eight years old and that they were his teachers. A woman named Ana Cecelia Rodríguez introduces herself as a doctoral student at the university in Tlaxcala, saying she has come here to learn from this community. There are also a few other farmers from the area, all of whom have been learning and teaching sustainable agriculture techniques in recent years.

Just as we're starting the slideshow presentation, several more people arrive. Eric suddenly stops translating and jumps up for a backslapping, joyous hug with his old friend Gabriel Sánchez Ledezma, who now lives and works on a butterfly reserve in Michoacán. After more welcomes and introductions, we finally begin the presentation about *El Grupo Vicente Guerrero*, the rural development group that these people established in the late 1970s, as their work with soil conservation gained momentum.

Now an official nonprofit, the group's work still focuses mainly on soil and water conservation: building terraces, planting vegetation to hold the terraces in place, digging water catchment ditches and ponds. (There is no irrigation here and rainfall is only about six to seven hundred millimeters per year, so careful management is crucial.) The group members work together to implement these practices in their own fields, and also to hold workshops for visiting farmers who then return home and teach others.

In addition to the basics of soil and water conservation, El Grupo Vicente Guerrero works on other projects, such as the following:

- Reducing the use of chemical inputs by using organic fertilizers such as compost and cover crops[3] and by practicing integrated pest management.[4]
- Improving nutrition by planting vegetable gardens and raising small animals.
- Saving seeds from native crop varieties, to preserve the diversity of corn and beans and other plants in this region. (For the past ten years, these farmers have been holding an annual seed exchange, where farmers from all over Tlaxcala and Puebla come to trade their seeds.)
- Reviving traditional cropping practices such as the "three sisters," i.e., corn, beans, and squash planted together in the same field. (This practice was largely abandoned at the outset of the Green Revolution, when farmers were encouraged to plant entire single-crop fields of hybrid corn to maximize yields. Such a system relies on pesticides, while the traditional diverse system minimizes pests and diseases without the use of chemicals.)
- Using traditional medicinal plants for health care, and keeping these practices in use. (The majority of the Mexican population will use medicinal plants before going to a doctor, so the preservation of this knowledge is very important for people's health.)
- Educating young people about the environment and conservation, because they will be the ones to carry this work forward in the future.

These farmers want to build local and regional markets as well, so they can sell crops directly to consumers and get a better price. (At present, they sell to intermediary buyers who drive through the countryside with trucks, buy up the harvest, and sell it to large companies such as Gruma/Maseca. Under such a system, the prices paid to farmers are very low.)

It would be so great if they could do a campesino a campesino exchange with the farmers from El Ranchero Solidario co-op in Chihuahua, I think to myself, *with one group teaching about sustainable farming practices and the other teaching about co-ops and direct marketing.*

All of Grupo Vicente Guerrero's projects are implemented using the Campesino a Campesino methodology, in which farmer-teachers called *promotores* hold workshops for other farmers, sharing the personal experience and knowledge they've gained, and teaching people how to become promotores themselves when they return home to their own communities. In all of this work, Adrian tells us, there has been a significant effort to consider gender equality, trying to ensure that these projects don't place the burden of additional work on women alone (as often happens in development projects). Gender roles are usually a topic addressed in the workshops, which are led by both male and female promotores.

The presentation ends with a long list of rural groups that are now using the Campesino a Campesino methodology, over a hundred in all. This has created a sort of network, in which farmers from all over Mexico and Central America gather to hold trainings, discuss the problems they're facing, and share ideas with one another. A group of promotores from one village will visit and stay for a few days or weeks at a training center like this one . . . some communities have even adopted a promotora for months at a time.

"This has all happened because of the complete failure of the government to address the needs of campesinos," Adrian says, "and so we've come together to advance our own alternatives instead. When we say sustainable agriculture, we mean an agriculture that sustains itself and has no need for outside inputs. This is one reason that seed-saving is so important."

"Are a lot of [external] inputs still used here?" asks Jan.

"Yes," he replies, "the government is still promoting chemical inputs through their extension agents and 'technological packages.' But

Direct Marketing by Small Farmers in
Central and Southern Mexico

Even though many small farmers in Mexico have raised the fertility and productivity of their land through sustainable agroecological farming methods, they still lack a profitable way to sell their crops. Local markets have been overrun by competition from agribusiness and cheap imports, while the Mexican government has dismantled its system of production credit, crop insurance, and agricultural extension that might have allowed these smaller producers to compete. Private investors in Mexico are unwilling to finance projects involving campesino agriculture, and the few loans available are for conventional, chemical-based production rather than the low-input model used by the Campesino a Campesino Movement.

However, one farmers' organization in the state of Puebla is currently working with U.S. investors to begin marketing its crops in the United States. This project aims to take advantage of NAFTA for the benefit of small farmers (whom free trade has generally excluded), beginning with a pilot project of thirteen fruit, vegetable, and grain growers in the small town of San Luis Coyotzingo. To establish such a business, the growers need an initial loan for basic infrastructure such as tools, greenhouses, improvements to their irrigation system, a packing shed, and a cooler. They also need political support to defend their historic water rights, as well as training in cooperative business management, post-harvest handling, wholesale and retail. These types of services are unavailable from either the private sector or the Mexican government, but recently a private U.S. investor offered to finance the project, with the idea of creating a niche market for sustainably produced vegetables from small farming villages in Mexico. The goal is for export sales to provide these farmers with a stable source of income, which will then allow them to begin selling in local and regional markets as well. In this way, the project would complement, rather than replace, the capacity to provide food at fair prices to local consumers.

One challenge to this project is that many people from the region have already migrated and will not readily abandon their other jobs and return to farming unless convinced there is adequate credit and a relatively stable market for their goods. Because these farmers are very hesitant to take financial risks and fall into debt, some sort of crop insurance may be necessary in order for them to risk borrowing money for any new project involving agricultural production. Although the community is situated along a major NAFTA trade route, another challenge may be the cost of transporting produce from Puebla to the United States.

In nearby Tlaxcala, other farmers from the Campesino a Campesino Movement are interested in building a factory to mill their own corn flour and sell tortillas directly to the public. In recent years, urban tortilla stands that once bought corn from the surrounding countryside have begun purchasing it for cheaper prices from Mexico's large grain corporations, Gruma/MASECA and MINSA, which import some of their product from the United States. This corn flour contains a mixture of industrially produced grains from throughout Mexico and the United States, resulting in tortillas of much lower quality than those made from traditional local corn varieties. Because of this, small farmers in Tlaxcala may be able to establish a market for "authentic," high-quality tortillas, which—by eliminating the intermediary grain buyers and processors—they will be able to sell to low-income consumers at competitive prices. Like El Ranchero Solidario cooperative in Chihuahua, this project has the potential to reduce migration and improve the livelihoods of farming communities in the region. But like any such endeavor, it will require initial start-up funds that are extremely difficult for small farmers to obtain, given the current political and economic climate. Yet only through such efforts will the Campesino a Campesino Movement, with its successful strides toward environmental sustainability, be able to achieve *economic* and *social* sustainability as well.

(See reference section for source material.)

Grupo Vicente Guerrero is resisting this, and educating farmers here to resist it."

"How do you recover the native seeds?" Denise asks.

"At first, we only knew of some seeds in the immediate area," he replies, "but then we did an inventory of the whole region."

"Is there a problem with traditional and modern varieties cross-pollinating?" I want to know.

He explains how they harvest seed from the very center of a field, where it's least likely to have received pollen from neighboring fields, and save that part for planting the next year. But still, Adrian says, modern hybrids and genetically engineered (GE) crops do pose a threat to the preservation of native varieties, and there's a proposal at the state level to declare Tlaxcala a "center of origin"[5] for maize and thereby prevent GE corn from being planted in the state.

Trevor is curious about new strategies for marketing crops directly.

"We're working on a proposal now," Adrian says, "and we're also looking for a way to add value by processing the grains ourselves and then selling them in local and national markets."

"How has the government responded to this movement?" Jan asks.

"Up until now, we've basically had no problems with the government," he says. "We're hoping to show them that there are campesino alternatives to development."[6]

The presentation is over, and Eric invites the four men who worked with him in the 1970s to come to the front of the room. They stand together in a row, and I examine those weathered faces staring solemnly out from under the brims of cowboy hats, thinking how these men were all in their twenties and thirties when Eric lived here and this movement began . . . they were *my* age!

Standing there with his old friends, Eric is eager tell us a more personal story of how this all began. "This is almost the entire group that traveled to Guatemala together," he says, "in a truck we borrowed from the Casa de los Amigos. They were all farmers, concerned about their own fields and harvests and the work they'd left behind, uncertain about traveling to a place where they'd never been and didn't speak the native language, not knowing what to expect. . . ."

With a smile, he recounts how they saw the ocean for the very first time and all went swimming together. When they arrived in Guatemala, the group was met by a very small indigenous man who had arrived to take them to the fields. *What's this guy possibly going to teach us*, they wondered, but when they passed a beautiful, extremely healthy field of corn, unlike anything back home, everybody stopped and gasped and exclaimed, "Whose corn is this?!" "Mine," said the man. They were immediately eager to learn what he was doing to produce such a healthy crop, and made the Guatemalan farmer repeat everything four or five times in his limited Spanish until they finally understood. "Campesinos will always find a way to communicate," Eric says.

When the group returned to Vicente Guerrero and started making terraces, at first people in the village thought it was crazy. But when the rains came and those fields didn't flood or erode, others started getting interested, and a gradual domino effect began. Over the next thirty years, these men wound up bringing their village not only soil conservation techniques, but also a health center, better roads, and running water. At times, they've received a little support from the government or from NGOs, but mainly this has all been led and built by the people of Vicente Guerrero themselves.

The storyteller in me is completely spellbound by Eric's tale, fingers going numb as I scribble every detail in my notebook. *What an amazing history we are encountering here. . . .*

Next, Gabriel Sánchez Ledezma shows us a short film about his work on the butterfly reserve in Michoacán, where the Campesino a Campesino methodology is being used as well.

The government passed a law to establish this reserve, Gabriel explains, without ever informing the people who lived there. They just woke up one morning and learned they were forbidden to enter the forest, which they relied upon for wood fuel and hence, for survival. So of course there was a lot of resistance from the communities, and the forest actually became even *more* threatened, due to illegal trafficking of forest products by loggers from other areas.

Eric says this is the "created contradiction" between conservation and rural development. It seems the two goals are at odds, he explains, because the government and NGOs have often removed peasants from their land in an attempt to conserve it. But the goal of Gabriel's group, ALTERNARE, is to find ways to overcome that contradiction and to achieve *both* goals simultaneously. "You can't think about conservation without thinking about the people," he says.

The members of ALTERNARE have created a training program in conservation, using the Campesino a Campesino methodology. With the support of three U.S. foundations, they have built a center and are training promotores from villages within the reserve. The first goal of this project is that families can support themselves and produce enough food, using sustainable practices that do not threaten the forest. The second goal is to conserve the forest by growing trees for firewood in the perimeters of fields, building fuel-efficient stoves that require less wood, and building houses from adobe rather than lumber. The villages have also managed to establish a "no-use zone" in the center of the forest, surrounded by a buffer area in which logging is banned but other uses are allowed (such as harvesting wild plants for food or herbal remedies and collecting fallen wood).

There has still been illegal logging by outsiders, Gabriel says, but now several villages have formed commissions to guard the forest, and this has successfully prevented logging. Now that local people have some access and rights to the forest themselves, there's an incentive to protect it from exploitation by outsiders. As the forest gradually recovers, those communities are benefiting from increased springs and water supply, and other villages are beginning to see this and to form their own commissions to guard the forest as well.

A contradiction between development and conservation? I think to myself. *Seems like the opposite, to me! It seems that if humans are included as part of the whole system to be conserved, and if they have control over their own natural resources and the knowledge of how to use those resources sustainably, they will naturally work to conserve them.*

So far, ALTERNARE has been very successful, and Gabriel credits this success to the use of the Campesino a Campesino methodology. A lot of small groups have formed within the past few years to identify their communities' most important goals and seek the necessary training to achieve them. This training, of course, comes from the shared experiences and trials and techniques of other farmers in the surrounding countryside. "A campesino will always listen better to another campesino," Gabriel says.

He tells us how every village in the reserve has started a tree nursery, and how the use of firewood has decreased by 50 percent with fuel-efficient stoves. Many people are also learning low-input farming techniques and cutting back on expensive chemical inputs, just like here in Vicente Guerrero. Apparently, erosion has decreased significantly, and agricultural yields in some places have already doubled! ALTERNARE has been successful from the perspective of the reserve as well, as forests are recovering and butterfly populations have increased in the last three years.

"Is the human population growing too?" I ask, thinking this might be another source of pressure on the forest.

"No, the communities haven't grown that much," he says, "because the men are in the U.S. and the women are at home."

I wonder why there's still a lot of migration, even with higher yields and the beginning of new microenterprises (like beekeeping and herbal remedies), which Gabriel says are providing a source of income to the communities. Obviously the situation is complex, and the story we've just heard is more of a "positive step" than a "fairy-tale ending." I really want to know more of the details and complexities, but everyone's getting ready to head outside now, so there's no time to ask.

We set out walking through the streets and into the fields, which are

Campesino Emiliano Juárez shows visitors how farming sustainably in Vicente Guerrero has ended hunger by improving water retention and soil fertility.

basically a series of wide terraces all the way down the mountainside. Making our way carefully along the steep road, we pause to talk and learn about the fields we pass along the way.

The farmer named Emiliano tells us that the main crops here are maize, beans, squash, oats, wheat, and fava beans. (The latter are grown for consumption, but also as a cover crop to plow back into the soil and enhance its fertility.) Some of the fields also have berms of fruit trees—peaches, apples, apricots, pears, *tejocote*—which help maintain the edges of the terraces, and provide another source of food for eating and selling. Diversity basically means greater security, in terms of people's diets and food supply, as well as the economic viability of their farms.

"Did the government have any role in this?" someone asks.

Emiliano responds that there was a time when the government tried to help by bringing in tractors to make terraces, but that such projects were poorly managed and ineffective, and now the campesinos have taken it into their own hands.

In one field beside the road, we stop to look at a small pond that people in the community have dug to catch rainwater that runs down the hillside. Rather than flowing down the slope, water is now channelled through ditches into this pond, where it can slowly percolate into the surrounding soil. This not only prevents erosion, but also increases the water supply for crops during dry spells. For big projects like digging this pond, a whole group of people usually gather at one person's field for a required community workday. This system is governed by social pressure, so if one person doesn't show up, he'll probably get a check-in call to see what happened.

This is another advantage of small-scale, locally run projects, I think. *When Eric tried to organize workshops for the villagers back in the 1970s and turnout was very low, he didn't have this type of "social leverage" to get people on board. But when the community **itself** has created and agreed to a certain arrangement, and when people all know each other and are bound by unwritten cultural codes of conduct, they are able to ensure that everyone participates.*

We stand and admire a beautiful lush cornfield, which Emiliano says was once so eroded that nothing could grow there. By using a simple tool called an A-frame to map out the contours, and then plowing in a special way each year to gradually build up the terrace, they've managed to reclaim this area for agriculture. He shows us the compost heap next to one field, and explains how they're also adding organic matter in order to re-create fertile topsoil here again.

Eric says a lot of these hillsides looked like "moonscapes" back when he lived here, just as deeply rutted and barren and rocky as the road we're walking on. I look down at the chalky brick-hard road, then at the rich soil and healthy plants beside us. It's hard to imagine that in just thirty years, farmers here have managed to reclaim hundreds of fields like this one.

Farther down the hill, we pass beneath a thickly forested mountainside towering above us so steeply that it looks almost vertical. This area was once getting burned and deforested a lot, Emiliano says, and the wild animals were leaving it. So in the 1970s the community designated it a protected forest and worked for a whole year to replant. It was very hard labor, with people carrying water and young trees on their backs from the village, using ropes to climb these cliffs, digging out the brambles, and making little mini-terraces to plant each tree. The ground was so hard that it broke picks and shovels, but in the end their project worked, and the forest is now dense and full of life. Even though they reforested with cedar, pine, and a few fast-growing exotic species like eucalyptus, those trees have created the conditions (shade, organic mat-ter, and retention of rainwater) that are now allowing the native vegeta-tion to come back as well.

Emiliano says he realizes that climate change is happening on a global scale, beyond the control of one small village, but that people can still do things to make a difference in their own microclimate. Even if rainfall declines in this area, the existence of a healthy forest means that whatever rain *does* fall will be well retained and utilized. The way Eric describes it, these farmers are still impacted by larger forces, but they've "lowered their vulnerability to the effects of climate change."

Most of all, they've lowered their vulnerability to food insecurity. "People used to go hungry here," Emiliano says. "The soils were poor, the forest degraded and rainfall low, but now it's gotten better."

On the opposite side of the valley, one of the farmers points out another forest that's been designated a protected area. They used to graze animals there, he explains, but now it's off-limits, to allow the forest to regenerate naturally. However, there's been a problem with people from *outside* of Vicente Guerrero continuing to graze their ani-mals there, which gets me thinking, and I take a moment to jot down the following thoughts in my notebook:

It seems that borders can serve an important function by allowing a commu-nity to manage its own natural resources without the threat of intrusion by outsiders, who would be less inclined to protect the local environment . . . right? Just like borders can be used to define a regional economy, to prevent foreign competitors from entering a market and undermining the local produc-ers. The whole idea of food sovereignty, it seems to me, relies on having some sort of "border" to convey the message that "we are a distinct people and place, and we have the right to control our own system of food production."

And yet, as we saw in El Paso, borders can also serve a discriminatory function. They may convey the message that "your resources and the products of your labor can cross this line, but not your people. The border is permeable when we want to sell our products in your market, but impermeable when you can no longer survive in that market and want to get a job over here to support your family."

So a border itself isn't necessarily good or bad, I guess. It's just a line on the ground, and depends on the meanings and rules we attach to that line. Instead of removing borders altogether, as some people suggest, perhaps we just need to reevaluate their purpose. Is the border there to define sovereign zones of resource management, or to separate two economies, or to block people's move-

ment? What can pass through and what can't? I'm standing here looking at a grazing-free hillside across the valley, with all these thoughts running through my mind. . . .

We leave the road now and hike down a steep path into the valley, where all the crops are grown for home consumption and are strictly organic. Synthetic inputs are expensive, and people cannot afford to use them here, on crops they won't be selling. Besides, one farmer tells me, they do not want to eat food that's contaminated with pesticide.

Nestled into this small valley are several healthy looking fields of corn and also amaranth, an indigenous staple that fell out of use during colonial times but is now being recovered. Nearby are several rows of cabbage and tomatillos, part of a new effort to grow more vegetables out in the fields. Emiliano passes around a stem of the herb *epazote*, not the kind used for cooking, he says, but for insect repellent and combating intestinal parasites.

I wonder how many other "weedy" plants on the ground around us are actually time-tested medicines, known and used by people in this region for generations. I think about how many centuries it probably took to discover those things, to experiment and gradually learn how different plants could be used, yet how quickly it can all be forgotten. Just a few generations, to lose something that was built over thousands of years . . . like knowledge, or soil.

"Have you seen a difference in people's health, with all these changes?" someone asks.

One of the farmers responds that there has indeed been a huge improvement, especially with the native fauna coming back to reforested areas and providing another protein source for families here. "I thought my children would never see hawks or eagles . . . but they're coming back now because there are a lot of snakes and rabbits," he says. "And the reforested areas also have a lot of wild medicinal plants, which people use in the village."

"How old is the oldest person in Vicente Guerrero?" someone else asks.

Emiliano thinks for a moment, then tells us there's a woman who's 105 years old.

After looking around the fields for a while, we all sit under a grove of trees as Camerino tells about his work back home in the Totonaco and Nahuatl indigenous communities north of Puebla.

Indigenous campesino a campesino trainer, Camerino Aparicio González shares stories of how his communities are organizing to retain their agricultural biodiversity and rich cultural history, which includes participating in national and international discussions.

"We believe we can only improve our situation if we organize," he says. Realizing that small farmer groups must work together in order to have a stronger voice at the national and international level, ten community groups in Camerino's area (representing about five thousand farmers in all) have united to form a broader organization called *La Unidad Indígena Totonaca-Nahuatl* or UNITONA.

"The primary objective is to strive for the autonomy of our people," Camerino says, "which requires the development of sustainable agriculture." The groups are training promotores and holding workshops about agriculture as well as indigenous history and language, traditional methods of governance and conflict resolution, and national laws related to indigenous and basic human rights. One of their main goals is to preserve (and in many cases, restore) a sense of pride and solidarity as indigenous people, a respect for the traditional values and customs that are increasingly threatened by outside pressures.

UNITONA is large enough to work at the state and national level, lobbying Congress to protect indigenous communities. They have succeeded in getting five indigenous judges into the state courts, and have composed a law to officially recognize indigenous people's rights in the state constitution. The group is currently working on a proposal for a new forestry law, to give communities more power to manage their own natural resources in the face of large mining industries and foreign corporations that often claim the rights to those resources.

In all this work, Camerino tells us, rural groups have become aware of the threats posed by free trade agreements. "All they do is displace our internal market, and that's what has impoverished the countryside, displaced our workforce, and led to growing migration," he asserts.

In response to the threats of globalization, UNITONA has founded a project for "responsible consumption and internal markets." They have also developed a plan to educate people about the effects of modern hybrids and GE varieties on native corn, and to promote a continued respect and reverence for this traditional staple. "As indigenous people, corn is part of our spirituality," Camerino tells us. "The sustainability of indigenous people comes from corn, and this is what has allowed us to remain united. . . . We are called *hombres de maíz*" (people of corn).

I am moved by Camerino's energy and devotion to these issues, and will always hold that image of him standing under the trees, speaking so passionately about his work, waving a leafy stem of epazote in the air like a baton, for emphasis.

It's getting late, so we climb into the back of one farmer's truck and ride bumpily back up to the village, where a delicious lunch of soup, pinto beans, rice, fresh tortillas, and *horchata* with freshly ground cinnamon awaits us. After lunch, everyone gathers along the curb outside the training center to say formal words of thank you and goodbye, before the little bus arrives to take us back to Mexico City.

Our short twenty-four hours here have ignited something in me that's impossible to explain on paper. I want to stay behind in Vicente Guerrero, to get its soil under my fingernails and the cracks of my skin, to live and work and talk with people, to stay here until I begin understanding the rhythms and daily reality of this place. . . . But the bus arrives, and we leave similarly to how we came, as strangers, catching only a brief glimpse through the windows of another world.

During the ride back, I chat with other members of our group about the advantages of community-led development work, and how it seems that a better role for outsiders is to *support* rather than to *lead* such projects. NGOs can provide grant money, journalists can spread public awareness . . . and of course these peripheral supporting roles are very important, but it seems like that's exactly what we have to be, if we choose to participate in development in a foreign place—more like stagehands, while the community members are actors on their own stage.

And clearly, people are doing an amazing job at that, I reflect, *building alternatives such as the Campesino a Campesino Movement and the co-op in Chihuahua. So should we just stay hands-off and stop worrying about the whole thing, since communities in rural Mexico are solving the issue of migration themselves, through such grassroots efforts?*

*I wish it were so simple, but I know it's not. Not if our governments' policies actually **hinder** community-based efforts, if people's resources are being mined by foreign corporations, if the U.S. economy creates a demand and a lure for Mexican migrant labor . . . not if all these factors make Grupo Vicente Guerrero and El Ranchero Solidario just isolated bubbles of success in a political and economic context that works against such things. So what is our role, then, as outsiders inspired by this movement and wanting to support it? What if we want to help support sustainable agriculture and viable economies in rural Mexico, so that people can continue living here? Is there anything we can do, from our **own** positions back in the U.S., within our own communities?*

The question takes root in my mind, twisting like vines throughout the rest of our journey, until an answer finally begins to emerge.

5

Oaxaca

August 5th

The next morning we fly to Oaxaca, a southern state with one of Mexico's largest indigenous populations and highest rates of migration as well. I remember reading about Oaxaca in the news last year, when riot police disrupted an annual teachers' strike in the capital and a months-long conflict ensued. Hundreds of social organizations around the state banded together to support the teachers' union, demanding the governor's resignation and a major overhaul of the political system in general. This new coalition called itself the Popular Assembly of the People of Oaxaca (APPO), and for five months its members barricaded streets and government buildings, took over radio stations, and held ongoing demonstrations and marches throughout Oaxaca City. It still amazes me to think of eight hundred thousand people marching at once, almost a quarter of the entire state's population! The police responded with more violence, arrests, disappearances, and at least twenty citizen deaths. This confrontation basically ended in November 2006, with the intervention of a federal police force and the arrest of many of the movement's leaders. Still, I am aware that tensions continue, and that APPO is planning its next steps. After reading about all this last year, it's striking to realize we'll be right where it took place, and will even meet some of the people involved.

One of the first things we see in Oaxaca, riding in a van to our hotel, is a small field of corn. Right there beside the airport, as if welcoming us to this ancient birthplace of *el maíz*, the region where corn was originally bred by native people thousands of years ago. Driving through the streets of the city, we pass a slew of billboards and political signs for the upcoming state election (*"Más infraestructura para los oaxaqueños"*; *"Vota PAN"*; *"Joaquin Morales: porque vivás mejor"*) and streetside walls that have become intricate collages of faded posters, peeling old signs, murals, graffiti, and layers of crumbling plaster and adobe, with decorative iron bars over all the windows. We pass a variety of small Mexican businesses (pharmacy, liquor store, shoes, PEMEX gasoline) interspersed among major transnational chain stores (McDonalds, Pizza Hut, Office Depot, Burger King, MailBoxes Etc., Sears). It seems odd to see those recognizable logos here, in a place that otherwise feels like such a different world.

Beside us on the road, a large army truck filled with at least twenty police officers or soldiers passes by. The uniformed men sit in the back of the truck holding rifles, several of them watching our van and smiling. Then more trucks of police officers follow, one after another, about a dozen in all.

Where are they going? I wonder. *Is this a normal thing, or is it because of the election? There's no march or demonstration or anything today, and the streets seem perfectly calm . . . so why this massive police presence?*

We drive past more stores, apartments, half-finished concrete buildings and weedy vacant lots, women selling flowers on the street, people walking with grocery bags slung over their arms, trees with large orange blooms, the state university, and finally the old colonial part of the city where we'll be staying. The cobblestone streets are lined with brightly painted tile-roofed buildings, more flowering trees, and old weathered stone churches. I now see why some people call this one of the most beautiful cities in Mexico.

*Itanoní, an urban restaurant working to preserve traditional maize
varieties by purchasing them from regional indigenous farmers*

For lunch, we head to a restaurant called *Itanoní: El Flor de Maíz* (The
Flower of Maize), where all the food is made with Oaxacan corn purchased directly from local farmers. At the center of the outdoor dining
patio are an array of sauces and spices, a traditional stone *comal* (grid-
dle) and a stone slab for rolling out tortillas, where two women stand
and prepare the traditional recipes from scratch.

After a delicious meal of pre-Hispanic Oaxacan dishes such as *tetelas*
(triangular pockets of corn masa with a variety of savory fillings) and
quesadillas de milpa (tortillas with melted cheese and squash flowers),
we remain at our table for a conversation with the restaurant's founder
and owner, Amado Ramírez Leyva. "You've tasted two varieties of white
maize today," he tells us, "one from the coastal lowlands and one from
the mountains at an elevation of twenty-four hundred meters. People
don't realize the extent of maize diversity in Mexico, so we are trying to
demonstrate it to our customers, by showing that even two varieties of
the same color can taste very different."

Each of Mexico's thousands of maize varieties has a unique identity,
he explains, depending on the geographic location where it was developed, the people there, and the particular traits of seeds they've chosen
to save and replant. For example, people in Zacatecas like softer food, so
their corn has soft kernels and a milder flavor. In other regions, where
coarser food is preferred, the kernels are of a tougher texture. Each variety is also adapted to the soil type, rainfall, temperature, and other environmental factors where it grows, so although modern hybrid corn may
be capable of higher yields than traditional varieties, it's not as well
suited to the tastes and diverse climatic conditions of the southern
Mexican highlands.

The tortillas at most stores and restaurants today have no identity,
Amado maintains. You don't know where that corn came from, or what
variety it is. In fact, most tortillas contain several different types of
hybrid corn, grown all over North America and milled at large processing plants. To trace those tortillas back to their original sources would
be almost impossible. With globalization, Amado reminds us, any input
from anywhere can arrive anyplace else in the world. So what does this
do to our identity and sense of place?

In an attempt to break from that trend, *Itanoní* is one of the few
restaurants in Mexico to still sell tortillas made from a single variety of
maize grown in a specific area. Amado has developed a relationship

Restaurant, Itanoní: El Flor de Maíz in Oaxaca serves traditional corn dishes made from local native corn as a way to preserve traditional corn varieties.

with four groups of indigenous farmers throughout Oaxaca who supply about a dozen local varieties of corn directly to his restaurant.

This is not just about crop diversity, Amado points out, but cultural diversity as well. Oaxaca is home to sixteen distinct ethnic groups and languages, each with its own long history and relationship to maize. Thousands of years ago, these people's ancestors began cultivating the native grass *teosinte*, deliberately selecting seed from plants with the best characteristics for eating. Gradually, they developed what we know as corn, a very different plant from its wild predecessor. While the seeds of *teosinte* fall onto the ground when mature, corn kernels have been bred to stay firmly on the cob, so corn cannot reproduce by itself but requires humans to harvest and then replant its seeds. This means that if people stopped cultivating all those varieties of maize, they would cease to exist! "It's like when you get married," Amado says. "You give up some independence, but what comes from the couple is more beautiful than how you were alone." In Mexico, there is a long-standing marriage between humans and maize, and that's what *Itanoní* aims to preserve.

Amado informs us that maize grown by small farmers in the mountains actually supplied Mexico's urban areas until the 1940s, when there was no longer enough to meet the growing cities' needs. So the scientists of the Green Revolution developed higher-yielding varieties, which are now used for large-scale commercial production and international trade. But that project was based only on yields, Amado says, with no consideration for taste. So indigenous farmers (who produce mainly for home consumption rather than the market) have continued to grow the old traditional varieties, based on their desirable qualities for cooking and eating. That's why so much maize diversity still exists today, he explains. But he lists three major threats to that diversity:

- **Free Trade:** Cheap corn is arriving in villages, and it's easier to buy it than to produce corn.
- **Migration:** In many villages, nearly all the working-age people have migrated, so no one is cultivating the native varieties. People in these villages have remittance money to buy industrially produced tortillas, but they don't have enough labor to continue farming.
- **Biofuels:** The demand for ethanol is growing and might divert production away from food corn.

"We can only confront these threats if many of us work together," Amado says. He's referring to farmers but also to urban consumers, whom this restaurant is here to educate. Amado's plan is to establish a chain of *Itanoní* franchises throughout Mexico, each one buying from farmers in its own region, creating a market for local maize varieties and a public demand for them to be cultivated.

"Do you think Mexico needs the modern hybrid varieties, in order to ensure enough food for the population, as *well* as the native varieties to preserve diversity?" I ask.

Amado replies that he believes we need both. This isn't about "getting rid of McDonalds," he says, but just allowing the two models to coexist, without traditional systems being wiped out either.

"What do you think about genetically modified crops?" Trevor challenges.

"I didn't want to get into that!" Amado laughs in response. "We have to solve many problems, such as migration, which is affecting everyone everywhere. Genetic engineering could present problems, but it's not as huge or widespread a threat. We need to address the biggest ones first."

Can the issues really be separated that easily? I wonder. *Even if they all stem from a common root, namely the entrance of multinational agribusinesses into the Mexican countryside? Can we really address certain aspects while ignoring others, when everything seems to be so interconnected?*

Leaving the restaurant and beginning our drive out into the campo, I ask Eric what he thinks about Amado's claim that domestic maize supply was inadequate to feed the urban population in the 1940s. Eric says he believes it's a myth, that Mexico actually produced enough to feed its population when the Green Revolution began. Localized hunger did occur sometimes, he explains, because people were too poor to buy food from other areas if their harvest failed, and because the infrastructure for transporting food was very limited. But those are problems of poverty and food distribution, not of agriculture itself. According to Eric, the intervention was completely unnecessary, and was based on the false assumption of an impending food crisis, and on the self-serving motives of the Rockefeller Foundation. But Amado, having studied agricultural economics in the Mexican university system, would not have learned that version of the story.

I can't help thinking, yet again, what a major turning point in world history the Green Revolution has been, and how the majority of people I meet are completely unaware of it. It seems that most people have never even heard of the Green Revolution, nor the continuing controversy over its impacts, even though it affects all of our lives every day.

With such a lack of awareness, I wonder, *what happens to the accountability of government agencies and chemical companies and agricultural research centers, to the public? Who's paying attention to what they do? Regardless of the pros and cons of the Green Revolution, it seems pretty clear to me that an ignorant population is a vulnerable one—particularly when that ignorance is in the area of our own food supply! Why isn't this important part of history taught in our schools?*

Meeting with activist Aldo Gonzáles of the Union of Organizations of the Sierra Juárez Mountains of Oaxaca (UNOSJO) about the struggle to protect local natural resources from extraction by outside corporations, and the connection between environmental issues and migration

Past the outskirts of Oaxaca City, we drive up winding roads into the Sierra Juárez mountains. Unlike the pine forests of Tlaxcala, the landscape here feels more like a jungle, a dense growth of succulents and ferns, vines, broad-leafed plants, mosses and lichens and all sorts of trees . . . so many brilliant shades of green. Eric says that most of the land we see is inhabited by indigenous communities who were once driven off the bottomlands and pushed up into these mountains by the Spaniards. The land here is actually very fertile, he says, but is suscepti-ble to losing that fertility if cultivated incorrectly. As we drive along, I can see bright green plots of corn growing on impossibly steep hillsides, surrounded by trees.

"Are those a threat to the forest?" I ask.

Eric says that many of these are actually sustainable slash-and-burn systems, in which people clear an area to cultivate it for a while, then move on and allow it to regenerate for the necessary period of about thirty years. By the time they return, the forest has completely regrown.

But what if migration stopped? I ponder. Would this system still be sustain-able? Usually, the problem with slash-and-burn agriculture arises when human populations grow too large for the land base supporting them, and people return to an area before it has fully regenerated. If everybody born in these mountains stayed here, would there be enough land for them to all sub-sist without degrading the forest?

Higher and higher we climb, passing through occasional villages with small houses and grazing animals, lots of little shops, oil paintings propped along the roadside to attract passing tourists; then through an area of somewhat bare and scrubby hillsides (the result of logging, per-haps?) and finally up to the village of Guelatao, our destination for the afternoon.

Unlike the other farming communities we've visited thus far, Guela-tao is also a tourist attraction. Along the main road are little cafés, lodg-ings, and souvenir shops, interspersed with brick houses, laundry lines and backyard cornfields. We get out of the van and walk up the steep main road, past a large plaza and ecotourism center. Beyond the main part of town, we head up a narrow footpath on the mountainside, past more small cornfields and a few houses surrounded by banana trees and nestled into the lush green vegetation. The afternoon rain clouds are already heavy, and a light drizzle begins as we head briskly up the rocky path. We're on our way to the log and adobe cabin that houses the Union of Organizations of the Sierra Juárez Mountains of Oaxaca (UNOSJO). This coalition of twenty-six indigenous Zapotec communi-ties has been working since 1990 to maintain their collective land rights, protect watersheds and water access, and prevent illegal logging of their forests.

We gather inside the UNOSJO building as a gentle rain falls outside. A cow tied up to graze on the steep mountainside stands at the open doorway, peering in with curiosity. It feels so peaceful and secluded way up here that I can hardly imagine police or paramilitaries ever arriving in such a place. Yet I know that even quiet villages in the mountains have not been immune to such interventions. Just two weeks ago, in the Zapotec village of San Isidro Aloápam, community members peacefully protesting the logging of their forests were attacked by paramilitaries, resulting in six deaths and many arrests. I realize that the idyllic

View of the Zapotec community of Guelatao from the headquarters of the Union of Organizations of Sierra Juárez with the Sierra Juárez Mountains of Oaxaca in the background.

setting through that doorway is also the backdrop for a tense conflict, a battleground where local people struggle with large, powerful industries over the rights to water, minerals, timber, and other valuable natural resources.

We have come here to talk about that struggle with community member and activist Aldo Gonzáles, who once served as municipal president of Guelatao and is currently a leader of UNOSJO. We sit in a circle in the meeting room, as Aldo speaks in a quiet, steady voice about the challenges facing this area.

Through the 1990s, he says, coffee was a very important product in this part of the Sierra, the primary and sometimes only source of income for many communities. Coffee farmers used to make an average income of eight hundred dollars annually, which was enough to support themselves since they produced food for home consumption as well. But after coffee prices crashed in the 1990s, (due to free trade policies and an oversupply of coffee in the global market), it was suddenly impossible to earn a sufficient income by growing coffee, and people began to migrate. About one-third of economically active people have now left, Aldo says, and this is having a serious impact on the communities. For example, there are no longer enough people to carry out the traditional *cargos*, or posts, to which village members are elected each year. (These positions include local judge, police, water committee, school committee, and mayor, and are part of an ancient system of governance that Oaxacan indigenous communities have practiced for centuries.) Also, women must now care for their families alone, and in addition to their usual work, must attend community meetings and take on the roles of their absent husbands.

I wonder how this has affected the societal position of women here, I think to myself, *and whether another side effect of migration has been a changing of women's status and decision-making power in their households and communities. This is something I'd like to learn more about.*

Another problem, Aldo explains, is the modification of Article 27 of the Mexican Constitution, allowing people to make private contracts and to sell or lease their ejido land to private individuals. He tells a story from back in 1994, when four nearby communities signed a contract with the Swiss pharmaceutical firm, Sandoz (which later merged into the large agribusiness corporation Novartis/Syngenta). The company provided villagers with microscopes and trained them to identify micro-

Aldo Gonzáles, leader of the Union of Organizations of Sierra Juárez and a member of the international coalition La Via Campesina, explaining the pressures of external forces on this indigenous region of Mexico.

scopic fungi from their forests, with a promise to pay over a million dollars to communities that identified a species of interest to the company. The problem with this whole arrangement, Aldo says, is that just a few communities signed a contract to receive payment for natural resources that *all* the communities share. In his view, such a decision should have been made jointly by an autonomous government or council of all Zapotec people who hold communal land rights here in the Sierra Juárez. But under the revised Article 27, each community can sign its own private contracts, which gives them more autonomy but also makes their resources more accessible for extraction.

UNOSJO has also been very concerned about the presence of GE corn in the Oaxacan countryside, Aldo says. The Mexican government placed a moratorium on the cultivation of GE maize in 1998, in order to protect indigenous varieties, but it seems that farmers have inadvertently planted GE corn that was imported as food from the United States. When UC Berkeley researchers came to this area in 2000 and discovered genes from GE corn in native local maize (suggesting that the two had cross-pollinated), they quickly informed the National Ecological Institute and the National Commission on Biodiversity. Scientists from those two Mexican government agencies came and conducted their own studies, confirming genetic contamination of native maize in a number of villages here in Oaxaca. But a few years later, Aldo says, they did another study and announced there was no more contamination. Now genetic engineering corporations like Monsanto cite that study and claim there's nothing to worry about. But in Aldo's view, it's not so simple. Even if the communities in that study had no genetic contamination, there's no evidence that other communities don't, or that they won't in the future.

"We're very worried," Aldo says, "because this is putting ten thousand years of culture at risk. GE corn is not a supercorn as people think, but is actually very weak, because it's genetically uniform and lacks tolerance for the harsh conditions here in these mountains."

To illustrate the need for preserving traditional local varieties of maize, he reminds us of the corn blight fungus that attacked the entire U.S. corn crop in 1970, and how scientists were luckily able to find a blight-resistant variety in Mexico, which they bred with the major U.S. varieties to make them resistant as well. If it weren't for such genetic diversity here, for all those hundreds of strains with tolerance to different pests and diseases, farmers might no longer be able to grow corn in the U.S. at all.

Have we really become so confident in our new technologies, I wonder, *that we think we can quickly create all those genetic traits in a laboratory, whenever they're needed? The idea of tossing away so much genetic material that already **exists** in the world, in hopes of just re-inventing it ourselves when necessary, makes me nervous.*

Part of UNOSJO's work has been to encourage the cultivation of native maize, in order to prevent those many varieties from becoming extinct. But with so much migration of working-age people, Aldo says, communities are no longer producing much food at all. With a shortage of labor and an abundance of imports and remittance money, a lot of the corn consumed here now is from the U.S. "It costs us 4 pesos to produce a kilo," he says, "but only 2.8 pesos to buy it at the store. So remittance money from the U.S. is actually being used to guarantee the dominance of foreign agribusiness in our markets."

Genetically Engineered Corn in Mexico

Genetic engineering is the use of modern molecular biology to insert genes from one organism into another, altering its genetic makeup in order to achieve new desired traits. Unlike selective breeding, which humans have used for millennia, genetic engineering allows the rapid (and otherwise impossible) spreading of genes to unrelated species, such as the introduction of bacterial or animal DNA into the cells of a plant. The U.S. Environmental Protection Agency considers genetically engineered (GE) crops equivalent to conventionally bred ones, yet the impacts of this new technology remain highly controversial among both scientists and the public.

In Mexico, GE corn is currently banned from cultivation in order to prevent cross-pollination with the country's thousands of maize varieties and their wild relatives. This diversity is considered essential to global and local food security, because it provides a "genetic database" for breeding new strains of maize, and because native varieties are well adapted to the specific conditions of the southern Mexican highlands. Yet diversity has already declined since the introduction of modern hybrids, and many fear that the spreading of transgenic DNA to local corn would accelerate that trend. Scientists from the biotech industry claim, however, that such "gene flow" would be harmless and in some cases possibly beneficial.

A lack of scientific consensus prompted the Mexican government in 1998 to place a moratorium on the production of GE corn. But in October 2000, microbial ecologist Dr. Ignacio Chapela and UC Berkeley graduate student David Quist discovered transgenic DNA in native maize kernels grown in the remote Sierra Norte mountains of Oaxaca, suggesting that farmers there had inadvertently planted GE corn imported for consumption. Dr. Chapela turned his findings over to Mexico's Ministry of the Environment and Natural Resources, which launched its own investigation and detected transgenic DNA in 63 percent of two thousand randomly selected maize plants in the Oaxaca Valley.

After an eight-month peer-review process, Chapela and Quist published their results in the journal Nature, but other scientists soon began questioning the investigative methods and validity of those results. (Some questioned the motives of these scientists, who worked for a UC Berkeley program partially funded by the major biotechnology firm Syngenta.) The editor of Nature responded to the controversy by announcing that Chapela and Quist's methodology was lacking and that the article should not have been published.

Since then, new investigations of Mexican maize have yielded conflicting results. The International Maize and Wheat Improvement Center (CIMMYT) screened seeds collected during a period from 1997 to 1999 and found no evidence of transgenes, yet Mexico's National Commission of Biodiversity announced in April 2002 that new data collected by government scientists showed genetic contamination of maize at 95 percent of sites surveyed in Oaxaca and Puebla.

In response, a global network of activists and rural organizations launched a movement called In Defense of Maize and held their first forum in Mexico City, where farmers expressed the desire to know whether their maize contained transgenic DNA. A coalition of organizations and Mexican biotechnologists began working with farmers to collect samples for their own independent study, taking maize from 138 communities across the country and analyzing it with the help of scientists from the National Autonomous University of Mexico.

A group of environmental, indigenous, and peasant groups also filed a complaint with the Commission for Environmental Cooperation (CEC), an organization created to handle environmental issues raised by NAFTA. The CEC commissioned a group of scientists (mainly with probiotechnology viewpoints) to examine the situation and write a report with recommendations. At a 2004 public CEC panel in Oaxaca, indigenous activists spoke for hours about their own experiences and veiwpoints, addressing the issue of genetic engineering not only in terms of biology but also indigenous culture and spirituality, colonialism, neoliberalism, and the power of transnational corporations. The CEC report, released later that year, concluded there was little scientific evidence of GE corn as a threat to biodiversity, but recommended—based on social, economic, and cultural concerns—that all GE corn imported into Mexico be milled and processed to prevent germination in Mexican soil.

Meanwhile, in 2003 and 2004, scientists from the National Institute of Ecology, National Commission for Biodiversity, and Genetic ID North America, led by ecologist Allison Snow of Ohio State University, surveyed 125 fields across the state of Oaxaca and sent maize samples to U.S. commercial labs capable of testing for very low concentrations of transgenic material. Their study, published in the 2005 *Proceedings of the National Academy of Sciences*, reported no evidence of transgenic DNA in native Mexican maize. The authors (including Exequiel Ezcurra, former president of the National Institute of Ecology, who had originally reported genetic contamination of maize in 2002) expressed surprise at these results.

Ezcurra said he had expected to verify Quist and Chapela's findings, but that any transgenic DNA present in 2001 might have since disappeared, thanks to a successful education program to deter farmers from planting imported GE corn. (However, the authors warned that their results should neither be extrapolated to other regions of Mexico nor assumed to remain static in the future.)

Contrary to this study, the independent investigation requested by maize farmers found transgenic DNA in 25 percent of participating communities in 2003. The results were reported via a press conference and detailed posters distributed to rural communities, where people used the evidence to continue their movement against GE corn. But because it was not disseminated through the usual channels of peer-reviewed journals and academic conferences, this study has been largely ignored by scientists and government officials.

Beyond the controversy over the presence of transgenic DNA in Mexican maize lies a broader debate about the use of GE crops in general. Proponents claim that GE varieties could benefit Mexican agriculture by reducing pest damage and producing higher yields while opponents question the use of new technologies to solve problems caused by earlier ones. According to UC Berkeley agroecologist Miguel Altieri, low yields and pest problems are the result of monoculture systems adopted during the Green Revolution, while alternative agroecological practices can reduce pests and increase yields without dependence on genetically engineered seeds and the corporations that produce them.

(See reference section for source material.)

How ironic, I reflect, *that many of the U.S. dollars earned by migrants and sent back home to Mexico are actually used to buy goods produced in the U.S., so that the money doesn't actually stay in Mexico, but flows right back across the border again.*

There are lots of questions for Aldo.

"Is that company trying to patent the microscopic fungi?" Leo wants to know.

"There's no mention of a patent in the contract," Aldo replies. "The industry just wants to see whether any of these species might be useful for medicines. But the problem is, they could easily discover something and patent it without us even knowing."

Denise, a teacher back in the U.S., is interested to learn about the school system here in these mountains.

"It's the same as the rest of Mexico," Aldo says. "There are primary schools in most communities, but they don't teach the values of the community. They forbid the speaking of native languages, change children's eating habits by providing unhealthy foods, and teach the students a different lifestyle so they grow up wanting to leave the campo."[1]

"Do people vote here?" Marilyn asks.

"Not in this election, because the PRD selected candidates without getting our feedback or presenting them to the people. We're not opposed to elections, but the system of political parties here isn't functioning. We indigenous communities feel we must look for representation some other way."

I remember reading an article about this, I think to myself, *about how APPO supported the left-wing PRD party in last year's national elections, managing to swing Oaxaca's majority vote in favor of the PRD presidential candidate and many congressional representatives as well. So I can see why people felt betrayed and disillusioned when the PRD recently divorced itself from the people's movement, excluding activists from its candidate lists and choosing party insiders who wouldn't carry such a strong association with last year's uprising. How are these people to vote, when they feel that none of the existing political parties or candidates actually represents them?*

"How has the government responded to your work so far?" I want to know.

"We have tried to avoid and minimize any confrontation," Aldo says, "but we are clearly being watched at both the state and federal level, and have received death threats. It's very difficult to carry out any social or political work in Oaxaca right now, and we have to be very careful."

According to Aldo, legislation is continually being passed that makes UNOSJO's projects and approaches "fall outside of the law." For example, many churches and village groups in Oaxaca have created their own small radio stations, in order to broadcast relevant information to people within the region. Unlike the mainstream stations that air a lot of programming unrelated to people here in these mountains, community radio stations generally cover local news, weather, health issues and other concerns affecting rural villages, all broadcast in indigenous languages spoken in the area. In rural Oaxaca, where other means of mass communication are almost non-existent, radio provides a cheap and relatively easy way to disseminate information among villages. UNOSJO is currently helping to start such a project, even though community radio stations are not granted federal licenses to operate. They exist under constant threat of being closed down, and with recent coverage of the social uprising and the activities of APPO, they are at even greater risk. So the new radio station is illegal and will have to be clandestine. Aldo explains this matter-of-factly, and I am struck by the realization that federal law would actually deem this man a criminal, this gentle-mannered and eloquent activist working so hard to protect his land and people.

"How has the popular uprising in Oaxaca affected people here?" Trevor asks.

"It affects the whole country," Aldo replies. "We tried to make this a nonviolent social movement, but the government has treated it like a violent guerrilla movement. There have been twenty-five deaths, over five hundred people apprehended, and six political prisoners still remain in jail. Many of the people detained have been tortured and sexually abused, and we're afraid that those who have disappeared may have been killed. The government is not only using police, but paramilitary forces as well."

"Has the government responded officially to people's demands, or only through repression of the movement?" Trevor questions.

"Before all of this began," says Aldo, "the Mexican government signed an agreement with the Zapatistas in Chiapas to protect indigenous rights.[2] This agreement was supposed to be translated into constitutional law, but the government hasn't kept those promises. The state government is unwilling to discuss our demands, and the federal government has been silent. Not only do they refuse to listen to us—they haven't even responded to the inter-American Commission on Human Rights, or to Amnesty International."[3]

But the hardships faced by indigenous communities here in Oaxaca, he reminds us, have roots deeper than just this recent conflict. They stem directly from the undermining of local markets due to NAFTA, and the opening of communal land to logging and mineral extraction. This part of the mountain is categorized by the government as a mineral reserve, and Aldo tells how a Canadian company has been coming into the area during the past couple years to explore its mining potential. Their investigations have already threatened some springs, he says, and people are afraid the company might install a pit mine somewhere nearby. But a lack of consultation or dialogue leaves the local people as mere observers to such developments, uninformed of the decisions being made regarding their land. (And because so many have migrated, these communities also lack the physical presence necessary to protect their lands from intrusion.)

Brian wants to know more about UNOSJO's efforts toward food self-sufficiency.

"We've been using the Campesino a Campesino methodology," Aldo says, "to encourage communities to grow their own food and to work with compost and manure. In the past, we tried to do large-scale projects that required more capital than was available, so now we want to do smaller projects for self-sufficiency at the family level. But there's competition from the government, which tempts people by coming in with lots of money for its projects."

These government projects, called Payment for Environmental Services, basically pay money to communities that set aside part of their land for environmental conservation. This program has been sponsored by the Mexican government since 2002, with support from the World Bank. The idea is that natural areas provide benefits such as carbon sequestration, clean water supply, biodiversity, and scenic beauty, which have been undervalued because they are freely available (unlike lumber and minerals, which have a monetary value). So the goal of these payment programs is to create an economic incentive for people to conserve the forest by setting the monetary compensation slightly higher than the "opportunity cost" of using that land in some other way, such as cutting down the forest, selling the lumber, and growing corn.

The problem with this approach, Aldo explains, is that environmental conservation is prioritized over people's livelihoods and survival. In order to receive money from the Payment for Environmental Services program, people must cede the use of land, forest, and water resources that support them. Many areas enrolled in the program are former agricultural lands from which the people have temporarily migrated to find work, but enrolment basically guarantees their permanent expulsion from the land. The program doesn't allow for the creation of agro-forestry systems that combine forest and food production, or other methods of sustainable forest management for the subsistence of local communities.[4]

I think back to Gabriel Sánchez Ledezma's story about the butterfly reserve in Michoacán, which seems to be such a good example of environmental conservation and poverty reduction being achieved simultaneously. *Has the government looked to ALTERNARE's success as a model?* I wonder.

Aldo says it's important to remember that a lot of people *are* defying these trends and resisting the many pressures to stop growing native corn, because imported corn is simply not as desirable for eating. It makes tortillas that aren't as soft or tasty as the traditional ones that people are accustomed to eating here, so this is the starting point for change. "We see corn as the basis for indigenous resistance," Aldo says. "But you can't just defend corn by itself. We need to conserve all of our resources: air, water, trees, land, and the rights of our people."

It seems we could keep talking with Aldo and asking questions forever, but the day is getting late. So we thank him for sharing with us and then spend a few minutes talking in small groups and looking around the main room of the UNOSJO office.

On the walls are photographs of the building's construction by community members a few years ago, some posters of native corn, and several news articles about the popular uprising. Some sections are underlined in yellow marker, highlighting the names of people who have been "disappeared," jailed or killed for their involvement with APPO. A tremendous sadness courses through me, reading these names and realizing that Aldo too could become a highlighted name on a page. Realizing that each of these names was a whole person, a family member, the life and energy and presence of a human being, just stamped out. Disappeared. *How can some people's deaths receive so much attention and investigation, while others receive barely any at all?* I want to stand on a high mountain or on a stage and shout out these names, so everyone will know how they died, so all heads in the world will turn for a moment to see what's happening here.

It's nearly dusk as we hike back down the rocky path, through the vibrant greenery and ethereal haze of mist and rain, back to the plaza of Guelatao. By the time we arrive it's raining hard, and we take shelter under the eves of the municipal building next to a large mural of Benito Juárez (Mexico's revered, first and only indigenous president, back in the 1860s, who was born in this village). I quietly watch a group of tourists examining the mural as well, and wonder how it feels to actually live in this community with a constant stream of foreign visitors.

"What do you think of the ecotourism in Guelatao?" I ask one of the UNOSJO activists who accompanied us down the hill.

He responds that it has the potential to be a good thing, but not the way it's currently being done. It would be great if people wanted to come here and experience actual life in this community, he says, to understand the daily reality for local people. But when tourists come and want fancy hotels and restaurants and places to dispose of their trash, it changes the nature of the village rather than helping to preserve it.

This strikes me as a bit ironic, because the idea of ecotourism is to help protect the environment in a place—which might indeed be happening here, thanks to an economic incentive to preserve the nearby forests and lake for tourism. *But,* I think, *what about preserving the **social** aspect of the environment, the way that people live in it and interact with it? Is it possible for ecotourism to leave that intact as well?*

It's already getting dark, so we thank our hosts again, wish them well in all their work, then make a quick dash through the pouring rain back to our van. Driving down the steep mountainside, I notice the words *Muera APPO* (Die, APPO) scrawled in black letters on the back of a street sign, and wonder who wrote them.

There is so much going on here that we can't see, I think to myself, *so many tensions and complex factors that we can't possibly perceive by just passing through. In some ways, I feel just like the tourists in Guelatao. Gathering sound bites and snapshots, trying to piece them together into something we can understand.*

Back in the city that night, we go out for a late dinner and finally walk back to our small hotel. On the way, we pass a procession of motorcycles, cars with honking horns, and people shouting and cheering with handwritten signs and posters.

"Have the election results been announced?" I ask someone.

But it turns out they're just supporting their party (PRI) and celebrating an anticipated victory for some of the state legislative seats in today's election. I wonder what the outcome of this election will be, and to what extent the story will differ when told by these celebrating urban voters, and by the disillusioned peasant farmers of the Sierra Juárez.

August 6th

Meeting with leaders of the Center for Integral Small Farmer Development of the Mixteca (CEDICAM) about the connections between soil erosion, sustainable agriculture, and migration

After breakfast the next morning, we set out for another day in the campo, this time to a region called the Mixteca Alta. But unlike the lush rainforest that we visited yesterday, these hills are covered with low, scrubby bushes and expanses of bare dirt and rock. Eric says the Mixteca used to be just as densely forested as the Sierra Juárez, but that all the trees were cut down centuries ago for timber and agriculture, transforming this into one of the most severely eroded landscapes on earth. The Mixteca also has a very high rate of migration, with almost half its residents living outside of the state.

Looking out the window as we drive along, I notice again that this isn't an area of large-scale or even partially mechanized agriculture, as we saw farther north. Just outside Oaxaca City, we pass a group of people cutting hay by hand and loading it into mule-drawn carts, and a man grazing a small flock of sheep on a scrubby hillside near the road.

We pass through the small town of Nochixtlan, another collage of crumbling adobe and painted walls; half-finished buildings with water tanks on their roofs and rebar poking up into the sky; rutted, once-paved roads; little shops; and the standard plaza and cemetery and old stone church with strings of colorful tissue-paper decorations. At portable grills along the sidewalk, women stand making fresh tortillas, weighing them on a scale and selling by the kilo to passersby. There's a *panadería, carnicería, tortillería, carpintería*, a couple internet cafés, a seed store, and several tiny shops selling imported products like TVs and audio equipment, shoes, toys, packaged foods, soft drinks, medicine, cleaning supplies, other typical drugstore stuff—and, as always, Coca Cola. That ubiquitous logo, plastered across city walls and billboards on every street we've traveled. It still surprises me to see these corporate-brand items here, seemingly out of place in the tiny adobe storefronts of this remote town in the mountains.

It must be garbage collection day here, because a bulldozer is driving around scooping up trash piles from the sides of the street. I examine the contents of those heaps through the van window with great interest. As one might expect, there's a strong correlation between the trash and the wares of those little shops—soda bottles, aluminum cans, styrofoam and plastic packaging, newspapers—all mixed with organic materials like eggshells, cornhusks, and citrus rinds. *You can learn so much about people's lives,* I muse, *by the things they throw away.*

We take a bumpy dirt road into the hills above Nochixtlan, stopping at a bare concrete building that serves as headquarters for a local farmer-led organization called the Center for Integral Small Farmer Development in the Mixteca (CEDICAM). On the dry hillside above the building are a series of deep trenches dug out of the earth, which Eric explains are contour ditches, designed for catching rainwater so it can soak back into the soil rather than flowing away down the slopes. This is a recharge area for the springs that supply Nochixtlan's water, but those springs have been drying up in recent years. In response, the members of CEDICAM have begun restoring pre-Hispanic contour ditches to catch the rainwater and replenish aquifers.

We all gather inside the building, which is similar to the training center in Vicente Guerrero. Chairs and benches fill the small cement room, and a dozen quilt-covered beds are stacked against one wall beside a collection of banners and posters. Jesus León Santos, a local

CEDICAM leader, Jesus León Santos explains how 400 Mixteca farm families are working together to restore forests and build contour swale terraces to improve groundwater and soil fertility in a region which the U.N. has designated one of the most degraded in the world.

farmer and leader of CEDICAM, greets us and gives a brief introduction to his organization's work over the past twenty-five years.[5]

Don Jesus was first inspired to do this work as a teenager, when a group of visiting Guatemalan promotores came to his village to talk about forest conservation. Later, when eight of his siblings left the village to work in big cities throughout Mexico, Don Jesus was determined to stay on his family's land and work to improve the environmental conditions and standard of living in this area. So he organized with a group of other local farmers and cofounded CEDICAM in 1983.

At the time, drought and extensive soil erosion made it very difficult to grow food here, and farmers relied on ever-increasing amounts of expensive fertilizer in order to sustain their meager yields. It's a cycle, he explains, in which people grow the crop just to get money for more fertilizer. At the same time, grain prices were falling, and many farmers found themselves with no choice other than to migrate.

The founders of CEDICAM decided to focus primarily on the issues of soil erosion and poor agricultural yields, so that this land could eventually support people again. They learned about soil conservation and organized community work projects to dig contour ditches and plant young trees by hand. Over the past twenty-five years, these farmers have built terraces to protect five thousand hectares of land from erosion, and have hand-dug hundreds of kilometers of contour ditches. Many report that nearby springs have more water now, and that some dried-up springs have come back again. In some of the forests planted twenty years ago, people are observing soil improvements and are already able to harvest some firewood for cooking.

CEDICAM currently includes fifteen hundred small farmers in twelve nearby communities. These people have successfully begun to reverse hundreds of years of environmental damage in their region, Don Jesus believes, and they've done it with very little money or technology or formal education, just farmer-to-farmer spreading of knowledge and a lot of hard work as a community.

Now CEDICAM's new president, Eleazar García, comes in to finish the presentation. He tells us about the organization's work to improve agricultural production using animal manure, cover crops, and worm compost, inputs from within the community rather than purchased from outside. These new practices began with a small group of farmers, he says, but others became interested as they started to see concrete results.

CEDICAM is also trying to address local health and nutrition issues,

Eleazar says, because even with improved agricultural production, people here continue to buy processed food. With an inundation of imported packaged foods into rural Oaxaca, and the cultural influences of migration as well, people are shifting away from the healthy traditional diet to one that causes more obesity and disease. (My mind goes back to all those little shops in Nochixtlan....) In response to this, Eleazar tells us, members of CEDICAM are working on growing fruits and vegetables for home consumption. "We introduce these ideas through workshops and Campesino a Campesino gatherings," he says. "It hasn't been easy, because not all the communities are interested in producing their own food and giving up things they buy. But as people see the improved health of those who have implemented such changes, it's starting to catch on."

"Have these projects been able to decrease migration?" Leo asks.

Eleazar says he hasn't seen that directly, but that every person we'll visit this afternoon has either been to the U.S. or had family members there, so we should talk to them and see.

Now he introduces us to Phil Dahl-Bredine, a lay volunteer from the U.S. Catholic service organization Maryknoll, who's been living here and working with CEDICAM for six years. Phil will be accompanying us this afternoon to visit a nearby community where people are actively involved with CEDICAM.

We share a quick lunch of homemade tamales and sweet, tiny bananas, then set out driving again along the rutted dirt road through bare chalky hills that seem to stretch on forever. It's hard to believe this area was once a forest. The whole landscape looks stripped naked, worn completely down to bedrock in places, covered in scars and abrasions like wounded skin. Deep ravines cut through the ground, where rainwater has carved out channels and carried away all the soil. In some of the roadcuts, you can see a thin layer of precious dark topsoil and the hard chalky mineral layer below. You can literally see what's being lost here, and what is left.

But we also pass the beginnings of new terraces and baby pine forests, which Eric says are just how Vicente Guerrero's now-fertile slopes looked one generation ago, and I take some hope in the knowledge that a landscape can come so far in just thirty years. But the difference, Eric says, is that people weren't migrating nearly so much back then, so there was more labor to implement these projects.

We pass through a village with those jigsaw-perfect walls of stacked stone holding up the hillsides, adobe homes beside small fields of corn, beans, and squash, a little stone cemetery, a radio blaring upbeat polka music from one house, earthen walls with brightly painted doors and windows, gardens full of cacti and flowers. Through the van window as we bump slowly along, I watch an old woman in a brightly dyed blouse washing dishes in her front yard; a mother sitting in the middle of a field with a toddler; men with long sleeves, straw hats, and sun-weathered faces riding on burros with wooden saddles; agave plants with flowering stalks as tall as trees . . . images you might expect to see on a postcard, but this is just everyday life happening here, far removed from the hotels and shops of ecotourism in Guelatao.

Just beyond the village, a farmer moves slowly through his field with a team of oxen and a wooden plow. Ahead of us, on the narrow and otherwise-empty road, rolls a large Pepsi-Cola truck. Such a strange combination, the plow and the Pepsi logo, side by side in this surreally barren landscape. . . . *Will that farmer go home later after plowing his corn-fields,* I wonder, *and sit down to drink a Pepsi? In which, ironically, the second main ingredient is corn?*

Farther along the road, we pass a man and a boy on the hillside, using a simple A-frame tool (made from three poles and a carpenter's level) to map out the contours of the land in preparation for new ditches. The man positions the A-frame on the ground so its two legs are level, and the boy collects large rocks to mark the spot before they move on. It was this simple technology that the first promotores of the Campesino a Campesino Movement used for implementing soil conservation and teaching others, I remember Eric saying.

We stop for a moment and climb out of the van to watch the two at work, and I walk over to the other side of the road and look out at the mountainside stretching down below us. Beside the road is a small field of corn growing in chalky gray-white dirt, powdery as a sand dune, and it seems unbelievable to me that anything could grow in such soil. Down in the small valley far below, the land is a green patchwork quilt of fertile fields, the result of rainfall and topsoil that have run off these hillsides and gradually accumulated there, leaving everything up here so desolate and bare.

Village of Saragoza, to learn from community members about their efforts to resist migration through sustainable agriculture and environmental restoration

Continuing down the road, we pass large rocks spray-painted with messages like *"Muerte al Gobierno"* (Death to the Government), *"Muera PRI,"* (Death to the PRI), *"No Tendremos Exito Sin Dios"* (We Won't Succeed Without God), and *"Viva APPO"* (Long Live APPO). My mind is swirling with all these images by the time we finally arrive at our destination, the village of Saragoza.

A group of about a dozen people of all ages gather by the road to meet us, and we shake hands and stand in a circle to make the usual introductions. People from this community have been working with CEDICAM for the past several years, taking steps to decrease their chemical use, improve their families' nutrition, and save native seeds. The afternoon's rain clouds hang above, and everyone's eager to show us around before the rain begins.

We walk down the road to a little stable where the oxen are kept in order to collect their manure in one place for fertilizer. Beside this stable is a heap of crop residue, which once would have been burned but is now gathered and used for compost as well. Near some people's houses, we stop to look at another composting system, where red worms eat the manure and turn it into rich compost for vegetable gardens. Beside the compost heap is a small greenhouse full of radishes, squash, epazote, and a new bed for tomatoes. Everyone stops for a few minutes to admire these healthy looking crops, and to marvel at the handful of squirming red worms that someone pulls out of the compost for us to see.

CEDICAM farmer, one of 400 participating Mixteca families, demonstrates animal manure collection used to enrich fields and improve crop yields.

Zeferino, a young Mixteca member of CEDICAM, in his corn field.

We then continue past the houses and out into the fields, pausing to look at a lush green plot of fava bean cover crop. "I rotate [my crops]," the farmer tells us, "because otherwise my yields go down. This area had corn before, now a cover crop, and next will have beans. I used to apply four hundred pounds of nitrogen and phosphorus here, but now just a tiny bit is necessary."

He also shows us a half-hectare plot of corn that will soon be ready to harvest. There's a surplus now, since most of his family is gone (one daughter here, two in Mexico City, and two sons on their own farms nearby), so he just keeps enough for his household and then sells the rest. Stacked in a wooden storage shed beside the field are bags and bags of his corn—white, red, yellow, blue—all local varieties. He explains how he must fumigate this corn, putting a little cube of insecticide in each bag to prevent it from getting moth-eaten. One of the women standing with us says that's dangerous, because then people eat the fumigant. Eric's friend Manolo explains that you can just coat the kernels with a bit of lime (which you do before making tortillas anyway) and it prevents moth damage just the same. *Perhaps this farmer will try it and then tell others if it works,* I imagine. *Campesino a campesino.*

Somebody asks about the white streaks on these corn leaves, and he explains that a bit of disease doesn't matter at this stage of the plant's development. If it had infected the crop earlier on, that would have been harmful, but now the cobs are almost mature so it won't affect production at all. "Some extension agents would see this and tell us to treat the problem with chemicals," he says, "because they don't want to see any pests or disease at all. But all these things go through their stages, and we know the insect and the plant can live together. Older leaves of a bean plant may have some holes, but the younger leaves are fine. So it's not necessary to spray anything."

This is integrated pest management! I think to myself with excitement. It's an approach that some crop scientists and extensionists have begun to promote in recent years, in order to reduce chemical use. Based on an understanding of insect and plant life cycles, it's possible to determine what pest population levels are acceptable, and at what level it's actually necessary to intervene.

*But this farmer seems to be an IPM expert already! Just like most people have been, all over the world, for thousands of years. How arrogant it seems to have ever sent so-called experts out to teach farmers, without considering their own expertise and pausing to see what **they** might be able to teach.*

We walk along a trail to some other fields, where people are growing rye grass as a cover crop. The soil is pale, dry, and very fine, almost like dust, and it's astonishing to me that anything can grow in it. But that's the whole idea. Rye, though nonnative, is a tough plant that can grow in dry and poor soils. It will be plowed back into the ground, which will increase the organic matter in the soil, until eventually a traditional cover crop like fava beans will be able to grow here again.

As we stand looking at the sea of delicate, pale-green rye stalks, Phil takes a moment to tell us about where we are. This is the ancient center of the Mixtec civilization, he says. Just over the hill is the town of Santiago Tilantongo, which was the capital city and center of Mixtec art and literature as far back as the eleventh century. Before colonization, Phil says, this area was all forests and terraces.[6] But the Spaniards cut down those forests for grazing livestock and brought diseases that drastically reduced the native population, so there weren't enough people to maintain all those terraces. The soil began to erode, and after a few centuries the Mixteca Alta has become one of the most eroded landscapes in the world. It's estimated that an entire *five meters* of topsoil have been lost here since the arrival of Europeans, Phil says, topsoil that took thousands of years to form. But fortunately, through deliberate efforts like cover cropping, it's possible to rebuild a soil more quickly than it would form by itself in nature. There is so much work ahead here, to restore the local environment so it can support people once again; but that's exactly what the members of CEDICAM have begun to do. Over the last ten years, they've already planted *two million* trees on more than twenty-four hundred acres of land!

Walking back along the path, we share a crackerlike homemade tortilla (very different indeed from others we've eaten along this trip) and stop to look at a field of corn where no synthetic fertilizer has been used for the past three years. The corn looks mostly green and healthy, but there's some unevenness to it, with certain areas tall and lush while others are smaller and paler. This is because they're having a hard time digging the cover crop back into the soil, one farmer explains. A lot of it remains on the surface, where the nitrogen is lost to the atmosphere rather than staying in the soil as fertilizer. Eric thinks about this, and replies that a common disc harrow could probably be modified so that oxen could pull it and successfully dig the cover crop into the soil, and the farmer agrees that such a change is needed before this new system can really work well here.

*What if agricultural extensionists worked on developing **that** sort of technology for small farmers? I silently wonder. Rather than focusing on chemicals and large machinery that are obviously inappropriate for this field we're looking at right now, rather than viewing oxen power as outdated or backward, what if they considered it an effective farming method that could be used in innovative new ways such as producing cover crop? Clearly the farmers here could benefit from a technological improvement to the tools used for plowing crop residue into the soil, but I doubt that most agricultural extensionists visiting this area would identify that as a priority.*

On our way back through the fields, a woman named Lucia tells us about the hardships she has witnessed and personally encountered, as a result of migration from this community, and how she has fought for the Mixtec language to be spoken along with Spanish in the primary school her children attend here.

A young farmer named Zeferino tells us about his experience migrating to the city, and how he was unable to make a living there and wanted to return to the countryside where he grew up. Now he lives

Mixteca farm women share stories with U.S. and Canadian visitors.

and farms back here in Saragoza, which he says is a wonderful place, if only people could produce enough to support their families and meet their basic needs.

When we get back from the fields, I walk over to the vine-covered veranda of one house and listen quietly as Juan Carlos films Zeferino's wife and mother-in-law talking about life in Saragoza. The older woman says she prefers life in the campo, where it's more relaxed and you don't have to work for money or constantly watch the clock. Also, she says, the harvest is a type of security. Even if there's not money for other things, they will still have food. Her daughter sits beside her, listening, as her own two children play on the ground nearby.

"What are your hopes for your little girl?" Juan Carlos asks.

"To get an education," the woman replies, and I wonder if that means leaving the campo. *Is that what her mother hopes for as well? Does anyone go to college (or even high school) and then come back here?*

"And you, what do you want when you're big?" the grandmother asks her little toddler grandson in a sing-song voice. "To go to the United States?"

Everyone laughs, and the interview is ended on a light-hearted note, despite the serious implications of her question. *Will* this little boy, Zeferino's son, be able to make his living here in Saragoza? Will he want to? Will things have changed by then, or will he join the swelling number of migrants leaving this area to head north for work? I join in the laughter at his grandma's joke, but at the same time, I really wonder.

The rain is beginning as we thank everyone very much, shake hands, kiss cheeks, and say goodbye. This time, I ride in Phil's pickup truck, listening to his stories of working here in Oaxaca for the past six years and seeing the impact of migration firsthand. He tells us about one family he knows, just over the hill from here, that had five young cousins working in the United States. A few weeks ago, Phil went over to their house and found the whole family in mourning because all five cousins had been murdered. Someone had pretended to befriend them, then killed all five to steal their money right after they got paid. It cost five thousand dollars just to bring back one of the bodies, Phil says, and the family had to sell their oxen and cart to pay for it. I know that hundreds of migrants die each year in the U.S. or attempting to cross the border, and I wonder how many other tragic stories were here today, surrounding us.

Thinking back again to Luis Alberto Urrea's *The Devil's Highway*, I remember how the bodies of the fourteen deceased migrants were flown back to Mexico at a cost of more than sixty-eight thousand dollars. Not to mention the thousands more dollars in medical and forensic expenses paid by the U.S. government, and of course billions paid to the border patrol to try keeping them out in the first place. Rita Vargas, a Mexican consul in California, asks one of the most poignant questions of the whole book: "What if somebody had simply invested that amount in their villages to begin with?" Listening to Phil's story, this question surfaces yet again in my mind: *What if even a fraction of that money were invested right here, in places like Saragoza, at the root of the issue?*

Driving back to Nochtixtlan in the torrential rain, we pass several streets that have become rushing rivers of muddy brown water. It's easy to see how erosion happens on the slopes here; with nothing to hold the soil in place, it just flows away in the downpour. And I now understand that until these hillsides are forests once again this will continue, with more topsoil lost every day in every rainstorm.

On the way back to Oaxaca City, Claudia tells us about the cooperative she visited a few days ago, where village women have created a processing facility for *nopales* (a type of cactus common in Mexican cuisine) in order to add value and sell their crop. Sitting around a table with ten women from the cooperative, Claudia says, she learned that every single one had a husband, father, brother, or son in Salinas, California, where Claudia herself lives. The region produces the majority of country's salad greens, so it's probable that every one of us has eaten lettuce harvested by someone who migrated from these very mountains where we are now.

The rest of the way back to Oaxaca City, I reflect on all that I've seen up until now.

Back home, whenever I pass fields where farmworkers stoop in the hot sun, I know that I'll always remember images of today, of the eroded Mixteca countryside and villages where families wait and hope for their loved ones to return alive. "Those workers didn't just appear from nowhere," I want to tell everyone who will listen! They didn't just materialize in the dishrooms and carwashes and front yards and fields of the U.S. They have homes and spouses and children and communities, this whole other life that's been left behind.

If more U.S. citizens could set foot here and get a glimpse of that reality, would their ideas about immigration start to change, I wonder, or their willingness to buy the products of migrant labor? And if so, what would such a change mean? Say, for example, that we turned to a whole new way of producing goods, either by mechanizing, as Dino Cervantes is doing on his chile farm, or by hiring only U.S. workers, or by returning to smaller-scale production that doesn't require a massive low-wage labor force. If our demand for migrant labor suddenly dried up, what would happen to these people so desperate for an income?

*On the flip side, what would happen to **us**, if the migrants no longer needed U.S. jobs, if they just stopped coming, if trade policies changed or more com-*

munities built viable alternatives such as El Ranchero Solidario co-op, to allow people to stay in their villages in Mexico? Who would harvest the lettuce and slaughter the meat and build the houses and clean the hotel rooms across America? What would become of all those goods and services everyone relies upon?

*It's the same question that has followed me throughout every day of this trip. And the more I reflect, it seems to me that we're in a relationship of unhealthy codependence. Not a win-win exchange in which "you need work and we need workers, so everyone benefits," but instead, a situation stemming from tremendous injustice—that many people who would **prefer** to stay and farm their land are having the rug pulled from beneath their feet (the "rug" being the local markets that used to support them) and are forced to leave and to accept poor labor conditions and wages up north; that thousands of U.S. workers in El Paso and other cities can lose their jobs overnight because labor is cheaper in some maquiladora south of the border, or because a desperate migrant is willing to harvest peppers for slave wages. . . . Sure, the migrant women in that maquila have expanded "job opportunities," but they also have poverty wages, unhealthy housing, harassment, and exposure to toxins. What sort of desperate situation would a person have to be in in the first place, for maquiladora labor to look like a good opportunity?*

A deeper look into the whole situation, such as we've experienced over the past several days, reveals that it just isn't so simple as economic theories would suggest. Beneath the surface, this supposed free trade of goods and labor doesn't look so free after all, not for the people who are denied the freedom to choose their own livelihoods, to work in their communities and earn a decent living. Not for the people who die at the border attempting to cross that fortified line, while the material goods that displaced their own livelihoods cross freely back and forth every day.

But that's just the reality of the situation, because the U.S. economy needs the labor, and impoverished Mexicans need the jobs.

Or do we? Do they?

*The only way to break this cycle, I think, is to change it from **both** ends simultaneously. For communities on both sides of the border to stand on their own feet, to live off their own natural resources and labor without extracting them from another place. In my view, El Ranchero Solidario cooperative is not just a solution for Anáhuac, Chihuahua, Mexico, but one that we could **all** learn from: a model of local, regional, and even national economies breaking the ties of foreign dependence and allowing people to make a living in their own communities, manage their own natural resources, and achieve not only food security but sovereignty as well; an economy in which the profits and the* *power rest not with distant transnational corporations but with the common people, the workers, the majority. (Although, as we learned in Mexico City, the forging of such local sovereignty will also require cooperation and solidarity at an international level, as the world's marginalized peasant groups come together to build a stronger voice.)*

*This is not to negate trade altogether, I think, or to ignore its potential benefits, but simply to reevaluate the **role** of trade, keeping it subordinate to the primary goals of local and national food sovereignty; to create a system in which trade is carefully regulated in the interest of those goals, in which the profits are reaped by the producers themselves, and in which those producers sell a diversity of goods in local and regional markets, rather than relying entirely on a single cash crop for export.*

*Questions that have been tugging at me all week begin to take shape into something new, a vision that seems to encompass all the things we've been hearing and witnessing throughout this trip, a theme that runs somewhere below the surface of it all . . . localization, autonomy, food sovereignty . . . something that is, at its core, the very **opposite** of NAFTA.*

Back in Oaxaca, Rachel, Brian, and I walk downtown to the zócalo and catedral, where tourists dine at outdoor cafes and an opera singer performs on the sidewalk, where there's no trace of the massive demonstrations and violence that took place here so recently. I walk alone under the cement archways of the state government building, trying to believe that *this* is where it all started, that the photos I saw last year of the teachers' strike and police and crowds were actually taken right here where I'm standing. It's so quiet and peaceful now. But I do notice some black spray paint remaining on one of the doors to this building: "Viva APPO," in bold letters. The zócalo may be empty for now, but this movement is clearly not over.

Walking back late that night, we pass the teachers' union building, with a huge political banner covering the entire facade, full of messages supporting APPO and criticizing the governor and President Calderón. Interestingly, up in the corner of the banner is a guy who looks conspicuously like Uncle Sam, giving orders to the Mexican leaders.

Back at our hotel that evening, I look through the daily newspaper and election results. It turns out that 70 percent of the state's population boycotted the election, refusing to support parties that they feel don't represent them. As a result, nearly all of the state legislative seats have gone to the conservative PRI and PAN candidates. Reading over my shoulder, Camerino comments that this is the voters' way of punishing the PRD for distancing itself from the social activists of Oaxaca. Thinking back to our meeting with Diputada Susana Monreal Avila, I can't help feeling frustrated at this outcome. Those additional conservatives in Oaxaca's state legislature will only make it harder to advance policies like the ones Susana talked about. But at the same time, if the PRD truly distanced itself from the local activists here, can you blame the citizens for withdrawing support? Still, I wonder if this will be counterproductive to their goals in the long run. But Camerino says the smaller municipal elections are coming up soon and that people are preparing to vote in those, where they feel it will actually make a difference.

I know I'll be looking up independent news sources and Mexican papers online, to stay informed of what's happening here. Especially once you've walked in a place and interacted with people, there will always be a certain connection and sense of even deeper concern. The ox-drawn plow, the Pepsi truck, those eroded hillsides and fields of lush green cover crop, the police, the zócalo, the weathered faces, calloused hands and earnest smiles of people we met today, will always make those news stories a hundred times more meaningful and vividly real to me.

August 7th

On the last morning in Oaxaca, we briefly visit a small nonprofit organization called the Center of Support for the Oaxacan Popular Movement (CAMPO), which is made up of professional consultants who support the region's campesino groups by providing training in cooperative management, marketing, and legal issues. It's important to have an umbrella organization like this to help small rural groups deal with the complicated paperwork of becoming official nonprofit organizations.

Walking down the road after our short meeting, I listen as Camerino and the director of CAMPO talk about the intrusion of large companies onto campesino land. They say that in the past, those natural resources were reserved for the subsistence of indigenous people, not for commercial markets, but now they are given away by politicians in Mexico City, who sign contracts with national and international companies for the rights to extract minerals, trees, even water. So representatives from the companies show up in rural communities, where residents know nothing about the deal at all, and present official papers from Mexico City saying they have permission to extract those resources. What can people do?

This is what they're up against, I think to myself. *This is why APPO exists, why the people of Oaxaca are angry, why this movement will continue, in one form or another, until something changes.*

Back in the city, we quickly gather our things and say a heartfelt thank-you and somewhat difficult goodbye to Camerino and Manolo. Then off we go again, through the streets of Oaxaca City and back to the air-port, passing more trucks of armed police and that same semiurban cornfield that first welcomed us to Oaxaca.

Sitting at the airport waiting for our flight, I overhear Eric talking about APPO and saying there are currently over a hundred people miss-ing, aside from over five hundred arrested. I ask him about the security of Aldo and the other activists we met in Saragoza and Guelatao.

They are at risk, Eric replies. But Aldo's strategy is to maintain a high international profile through the Vía Campesina, so that if he were imprisoned, there would be a major international campaign to free him, especially in Europe. That's his only real form of security.

Thinking of Aldo Gonzáles, with that calm strong voice and unhesi-tant devotion to his work, and then remembering articles I've read about police beatings and torture of citizens here, is too much to han-dle. *Must people who speak out to protect their land and livelihoods always work under the threat of attack?* My heart is heavy as we board our plane and lift into the sky over Oaxaca, but I leaf through the pages of my notebook for reminders of the many inspiring and successful efforts we've seen underway in the last ten days.

Perhaps this is what everyone has to do, I think—*Aldo, Phil, Camerino, all of us—to stop ourselves from dwelling on the barriers and dangers and tragedies, to instead shift our focus toward the growing energy and progress that's being made, to join together and just keep moving.*

Back in Ciudad Juárez, we are delayed at the airport due to some fine-print customs regulations. So instead of riding a bus as planned, we get the experience of *walking* across the border, over one of those bridges where hundreds of people go to and from work every day. We grab our luggage, skirt through the rows of semitrucks lined up at the border checkpoint, and step out across the chain-link–covered walkway of the bridge.

There's an endless line of cars in both directions, a stream of head-lights stretching on forever. The sky is gradually darkening over the Rio Grande, a smoggy pink sunset, behind the flags of the U.S. and Mexico flapping side by side at the middle of the bridge. It seems an appropri-ate way to end our journey, walking across this bizarre line. *It's so easy for us,* I keep thinking. *People risk their lives every single day to cross this boundary, to do what we're doing right now.*

But I know the complex issues of migration cannot be fully addressed here at the border. To address them, we need to look farther south, to the countryside of Chihuahua and Tlaxcala and Oaxaca and all of Mexico, where people are leaving because government policies and eco-nomic realities are forcing them out. We need to look north also, to the immigration laws, trade agreements, production systems, and consumer practices that are part of that whole system. We must look back into history, to find the roots of these current realities. And then, most importantly, we must look forward, into a future that has yet to be writ-ten, and that every one of us has the power to help write.

Epilogue

*Update on Mexico–U.S. migration, the Farm Bill, NAFTA,
and immigration policy*

Since returning home from this trip one year ago, I've continued to follow issues related to NAFTA, the U.S.-Mexico border, migration, labor, and agricultural policy in general. Though it often seems little has changed, a few important developments are worth discussing.

The most recent U.S. Farm Bill, passed in May 2008, retained massive subsidy programs for corn and other commodity crops, prompting governments around the world to accuse the United States of violating WTO rules and inhibiting further world trade negotiations. Meanwhile, NAFTA has now entered its final stage, with the elimination of all trade barriers (and in theory, all trade-distorting subsidies) for agricultural products. Even though most tariffs had actually been removed years ago, thousands of protestors gathered at the border and in Mexico City this past January, demanding renegotiation of NAFTA and a renewal of public support for the countryside. And although the presidents of all three countries continue to applaud the treaty, the Council of the Americas (a protrade business group in Washington, D.C.) reports that public opposition to free trade is growing. In a recent *Wall Street Journal*–NBC News poll, six out of ten Republican voters responded that free trade has hurt the U.S., and in a 2007 poll by Mund Americas, two out of three Mexican respondents voiced disapproval of the trade agreement. (This is a reversal from ten years ago, when a similar ratio voiced approval.)[1]

Supporters of NAFTA claim that unrealistic expectations of the trade agreement have caused people in both countries to feel disappointed, and that ongoing poverty is actually the result of failed government policies and larger economic trends, rather than free trade. Yet today, more policy makers are beginning to respond to the growing tide of public opposition. Currently pending before Congress is the NAFTA Accountability Act, which would require the U.S. to withdraw from the agreement unless specific conditions are met, including renegotiation of the agriculture chapter and improved conditions in the border zone. Jeff Faux, founding president of the Economic Policy Institute, believes that pulling out of NAFTA at this point would be impossible, but that the U.S. should support a $100-billion development fund to stimulate job growth in Mexico. (This is similar to the European Union's approach, which successfully prevented large flows of displaced migrant workers after international borders were opened to trade).[2]

Contrary to such recommendations, U.S. immigration policy remains focused on enforcement, attempting to seal shut the U.S.-Mexico border while paying little attention to the driving forces of rural poverty and migration. The Department of Homeland Security is rushing to complete its goal of six hundred seventy miles of new fencing along the border by the end of December, after which the agency will transition to new leadership and its future course remains to be seen.[3]

At present, the Center for Immigration Studies (CIS) credits stricter immigration enforcement as the main reason for an apparent decline in the illegal immigrant population in recent months. Mexico's central bank reports that remittances have been falling, and a new CIS study based on Census Bureau data suggests that the U.S. undocumented population may have decreased by 11 percent (over one million people) between August 2007 and May 2008. Analysts also attribute this change to a slowdown in the economy (particularly the construction industry, which employs about 22 percent of Mexican workers in the U.S.). The CIS report has received some criticism, however, based on the difficulty of counting illegal migrants, and the possibility that increased enforcement has simply driven undocumented residents further into hiding, so that they fail to show up on government surveys.[4]

But even if heightened security and fencing *has* helped stem migration, we still must ask ourselves: Is this a humane or sustainable solution? Will closing this wound at its surface bring about full recovery, even if a deadly infection continues to fester below the skin?

Overview of the Global Food Crisis and Mexican Tortilla Crisis

The plight of Mexico's most marginalized citizens has indeed worsened over the past year, with rising tortilla prices and the emergence of a worldwide food crisis. In many countries, grain prices have doubled or tripled since 2007, spurring massive riots and protests across the globe as people find themselves unable to feed their families. Ironically, many of those threatened by the crisis are farmers themselves, who receive little to none of the higher prices paid by consumers. Windfall profits are reaped by intermediaries; even in the few cases in which farmers receive higher prices for their crops, they too must *pay* higher prices for food, fuel, and fertilizer. Analysts have attributed the crisis to rising oil prices (which increase the cost of fertilizer and of transporting food), adverse weather conditions, and diversion of cropland for agrofuel production.[5]

When Mexican corn prices rose 60 percent in early 2007, analysts initially blamed the situation on a grain shortage due to agrofuels, specifically the diversion of U.S. corn to ethanol production. But later investigations actually discovered large supplies of corn in industry warehouses, where grain brokers and agribusiness corporations had been storing it, waiting to see how high prices would continue to rise. Even though Mexican corn stocks were at record highs, such hoarding activity created an artificial shortage that boosted prices in Mexico far above international prices. The main actors in this speculation were four large transnational companies—Cargill, Agroinsa, Maseca/Archer Daniels Midland, and Minsa/Arancia Corn Products International— which are the main buyers of Mexican corn and the main importers of U.S. corn into Mexico. Generous subsidies and a virtual monopoly on processing, transport, and storage facilities enabled these companies to purchase corn in early 2006 and release it months later at more than double the original price.* As people struggled to afford food, Archer Daniels Midland's profit in 2007 soared from $363 million to $517 million.[6]

---

* These corporations were not only trying to increase their profits but also to capture more of Mexico's corn flour and tortilla market, about half of which is controlled by industrial processors and half by traditional small-scale millers. As market prices rose, the corporations began offering relatively cheap corn to industrial tortilla companies, which could then flood the market with their own tortillas

This suggests a deeper (and less often cited) origin of the tortilla crisis, namely Mexico's dependence on a few large corporations for most of its food supply, and the elimination of programs that once regulated the market to prevent sudden price fluctuations for basic foods. Since the 1980s, such changes have taken place not only in Mexico but throughout the world, leaving millions of small farmers without access to the domestic markets they once supplied. Many have switched their production to agroexport crops such as coffee and cacao beans, generating income with which to buy basic foods for their families. But with rising food prices and the inherent volatility of global markets for luxury goods, this system has left small farmers more vulnerable to the economic and climate-based factors on which the food crisis is now blamed. According to Laura Carlsen of the Center for International Policy (CIP) Americas Program, such overall changes in the global food system (i.e., domination by a few large companies, dependence on international markets for basic food needs, and the loss of national systems to stabilize prices) lie at the root of both the Mexican tortilla crisis *and* the global food crisis, while the usual explanations, based on oil prices, climate, and agrofuels, ignore those underlying structural factors that created such instability in the first place.[7]

Governments and industries have generally turned a blind eye to these aspects of the food crisis, however, emphasizing instead a need for greater agricultural output and trade. In Mexico, President Calderón responded to the crisis by eliminating all tariffs for basic staple foods, which the National Front of Legislators from the Rural Sector argues will only benefit large private importers (who reap greater profits due to the removal of tariffs) while failing to attack the roots of the problem. Calderón also announced a temporary price freeze for more than 150 food products, but the list excludes traditional staples and applies only to processed foods, which are already contributing to serious health problems and rising obesity throughout the country.[8]

The International Assessment of Agricultural Knowledge, Science, and Technology for Development

In June 2008, representatives from 181 countries gathered to discuss the food crisis at the FAO World Food Summit in Rome, where they

---

and undercut the comparatively higher prices of traditionally made tortillas. Ana de Ita, *Fourteen Years of NAFTA and the Tortilla Crisis*, Interhemispheric Resources Center Americas Program, January 10, 2008, http://americas.irc-online.org/am/4879.

drafted a declaration calling for more emergency food aid, trade liberalization, higher crop yields in developing countries, assistance to small farmers to increase production and market access, and further investigation of biofuel production in terms of global food security. Many proposals at the FAO summit focused on expanding trade and boosting agricultural yields, despite a recent report from the *Economist* stating that "in most places there are no absolute shortages." The July 2008 G8 summit in Japan produced similar recommendations, with leaders from the G8 countries promoting biotechnology and increased trade as solutions to the food crisis, while ignoring the issue of speculation by major traders and transnational corporations. In the words of farmer and activist Yoshitaka Mashima, "We do not understand why the G8 leaders pretend to solve the food crisis with more free trade, while it is the liberalization of agriculture and food markets that continues to lead us to the current crisis. People need to eat local food to protect themselves from the instability of world markets."[9]

Representatives from small farmer organizations around the world have been holding gatherings to discuss the crisis and produce their own set of analyses and recommendations as well, calling for the removal of agriculture from free trade agreements, and the re-creation of national food economies that trade minimally while focusing primarily on domestic production. Their recommendations echo those of the *Chilpancingo Declaration*, written by a group of Mexican farmer organizations in February 2007. The declaration calls for a termination of subsidies to corporate producers and processors, renegotiation of the agriculture chapter of NAFTA, credit programs to create campesino-owned corn storage and distribution businesses, a floor price for corn that compensates farmers for the costs of production, and government regulation of the price and supply of basic foods. The Chilpancingo authors and La Vía Campesina maintain that with such policies, small farmers could easily produce enough—at an affordable and stable price—to feed the world. (At the same time they would also be creating jobs, cooling the planet, improving people's health, and protecting communities and traditional cultures.)[10]

In April 2008, a similar conclusion was drawn by the International Assessment of Agricultural Knowledge, Science, and Technology for Development (IAASTD), a major four-year effort to assess global agriculture and evaluate its potential for reducing hunger and poverty, improving rural livelihoods, and facilitating sustainable development. (Some have called this the Intergovernmental Panel on Climate Change [IPCC] of agriculture.) Sponsored by several United Nations agencies and the World Bank, the project included hundreds of participants from the scientific community, NGOs, the private sector, producers, consumers, international agencies, and governments from more than one hundred countries around the world. While past assessments of world agriculture have tended to represent a single perspective, government, or interest group, this one adopted a very holistic approach, addressing modern science and technology along with local and traditional knowledge, and considering not only food output, but the social and ecological functions of agriculture as well.[11]

While the final IAASTD report applauds the achievements of modern agricultural development in raising yields, it also states that this approach has been too narrow, producing an unequal distribution of benefits and a host of negative social, heath, and environmental side effects that must now be addressed. According to the executive summary, "business as usual is no longer an option." With climate change, population growth, and current methods of food production, the authors warn that the world is likely to reach a crisis in the coming years, and that to avert such a crisis we must end subsidies that encourage unsustainable practices and begin moving instead toward agroecological farming. The report criticizes the consolidation of power by multinational corporations that dominate world seed and fertilizer markets, and recommends greater access by small-scale farmers to land, credit, seeds, natural resources, local and international markets, and the value-share captured in those markets. It also calls for more collaboration between scientists and farming communities in defining the agricultural research agenda, and for rural development that promotes farmers' rights to manage their own soils, water, crop diversity, pests, disease vectors, and natural resources.

Although the IAASTD authors do not reject agricultural trade on principle, they state that current trade policies have harmed small-scale producers by opening developing-country markets before the basic institutions and infrastructure to handle such trade are in place. They recommend that these countries be granted special treatment in trade negotiations, allowing them to protect poor consumers and small-scale farmers, and to pursue food security and development goals above all. The report also voices concern about agrofuel production, stating that it competes for cropland, has displaced farmers from their land, drives up food prices, and has not yet been proven as an environmentally or socially sustainable technology.

But the most controversial aspect of the report has been its treatment of modern biotechnology. While the authors acknowledge the potential of genetic engineering to contribute to global food supply, they reject biotechnology as a "quick technological fix" and state that many of the environmental, human health, and economic risks and benefits are still unknown, that assessment of the new technology lags behind development, and that "uncertainty on benefits and harms is unavoidable." They criticize the industry's use of intellectual property rights, saying it attracts investment but also drives up costs, concentrates the ownership of agricultural resources, inhibits independent or public research, and undermines local farming practices such as seed saving and exchange, which enhance food security.

Such claims raised a heated debate among the IAASTD contributors, prompting representatives from Monsanto and Syngenta (two major biotech firms) to withdraw from the project altogether. The industry representatives claimed their input was being underrepresented and that the final draft of the report was overly cautious about the risks of biotechnology while downplaying the benefits. Following the withdrawal of these participants, *Science* and *Nature Biotechnology* magazines both published articles questioning the credibility of the report, and an editorial in *Nature* argued that the industry's withdrawal undermined the credibility of not only IAASTD but of the biotech industry and its ability to engage with critics as well. Because the report's critical approach toward biotechnology, biofuels, and trade liberalization runs contrary to key foreign policy objectives and corporate allegiances, the governments of the U.S., Australia, and Canada have thus far refrained from endorsing it.[12]

Personal reflection on the issues and alternatives presented in this book, and how they are connected to our own lives

Reading about these issues during the months following our trip, I began to notice that the factors driving migration from the Mexican countryside were the same ones driving up global food prices, and that the alternatives to migration that we witnessed in Mexico (such as the cooperative grocery and the Campesino a Campesino Movement) are the same solutions being proposed by groups like La Vía Campesina as alternatives to the global food crisis. I also began to notice that these same underlying problems and grassroots solutions extended beyond Mexico, seeming to apply everywhere I turned, in every news report and article and conversation. I began to draw more connections and notice more patterns.

In the months following our return, I've also continued thinking about how these issues manifest themselves in our own lives, and what we can do about them. For middle-class Americans like myself, the food crisis and the plight of migrant workers may seem far away, but I've begun to see they are not. Walking through the grocery store, I wonder how much of that food would disappear from the shelves, or what it would cost, if our country's undocumented workers were all sent home. Ordering at a downtown café, I wonder whose hands picked those vegetables, whether he or she might soon be deported, whether returning will be worth the risk. Typing this book, I wonder how many of my computer's electronic components were manufactured by young Mexican women in maquiladora assembly lines, and whether the book will be printed on trees logged from indigenous communities in Oaxaca, where people struggle against major transnational lumber and paper companies for the preservation of their land.

And I think about alternatives. I try to imagine a system in which our natural resources are valued and protected, in which every person can afford a healthy diet, in which farmers receive a stable and adequate income, food supply is secure (even in the face of drought or rising oil prices), and people are able to stay with their families in their communities if they so choose. I try to imagine what such a system would look like, and what comes to mind, every time, is the idea Guillermo Glenn proposed in El Paso on the first day of our trip: autonomous communities, local economies, living within our means.

This makes sense to me when I consider what would happen to us (or to *anyone*, for that matter, even those remote villages up in the Oaxacan mountains!) if our lifeline of mass-manufactured, packaged, imported products were to dry up. What would happen if oil prices rose so high that it was no longer profitable to ship fresh tomatoes from Sinaloa to Chicago? What would happen to entire communities producing nothing but cacao beans, if a worldwide recession sent the demand for chocolate plummeting?

If we truly want to end poverty for everyone, I believe we must also ask ourselves: What would happen if assembly line workers around the world *did* create other opportunities for themselves, and there was no longer a supply of destitute people willing to take low-paying, unhealthy manufacturing jobs? What would happen if every rural community in

Mexico built a local grocery store, and all the farmers began selling goods in those stores, rather than migrating north to stoop in the hot sun harvesting peppers all day?

If this happened, we *too* would have to start building local stores, where people could buy food directly from farmers, at appropriate prices for everyone. We *too* would have to start creating more diverse, small-scale farms that don't require a crew of underpaid laborers to perform the same backbreaking task day after day. We too would have to abandon the assembly line and revive the skill of manufacturing goods from locally available materials, as artisans and craftspeople have done for millennia. We would have to redesign our urban spaces. We would have to consume less and reuse more.

Pondering these things, I have come to realize that the changes necessary in rural Mexico, in order to address the migration crisis there, are tied to necessary changes in the rest of the world; and that by pursuing such change in our own lives, *we can actively support* those who are struggling to resist migration and to survive in their communities in Mexico.

These are the alternatives to building a fence. These are the new possibilities that many people around the world are already bringing to fruition, and that we too have the choice to pursue.

Dori Stone
August 7, 2008

Appendix: A Guide to Action

There are many actions we can take, in our everyday lives, to address the issues raised in this book. Here are a few places to start.

INVESTIGATE how the goods you use and consume on a daily basis are produced. How are the workers treated? What are the environmental impacts? How far were the goods transported? Take the time to research and know what your dollars are supporting, and to learn about the range of options that are available.

- "Sweatshop-free" clothing labels ensure worker rights and fair wages.
- Purchasing goods second-hand is another way to avoid supporting exploitative sweatshop operations.
- Small local businesses and cooperatives are an alternative to large transnational chain stores, that are consolidating control over the food system and pushing small-scale producers out of business.

ADJUST your food consumption and purchasing practices to support farmworker rights, small-scale operations, and the responsible use of natural resources.
- Organic agriculure protects farmworkers (and you!) from exposure to dangerous pesticides.

- "Social justice" labels are becoming more common, as organizations like the Food Alliance establish certification systems for fair labor standards. Even when no certification is available, purchasing food directly from growers allows you to gain familiarity with the farms and to ask about their labor practices.
- Fair trade brands of coffee, tea, bananas, chocolate, and other imported products guarantee a fair price and improved livelihood for the producers.
- Direct-marketing sales (from CSAs, farmers' markets, roadside stands, etc.) provide farmers with a larger share of the profit for their goods, as do sales of whole, unprocessed, unpackaged foods.
- By learning growing seasons in the place where you live, you can avoid out-of-season produce imported from large agroexport operations in Mexico and other parts of Latin America, where labor standards are exceptionally low and higher rates of pesticide use (including chemicals that are banned in the United States) are common.
- Businesses pay attention to consumer demand. Grocery stores, cafeterias, and restaurants often respond to customer requests to carry local, organic, and fair trade products. Ask them!

This may sometimes cost more, but ask yourself how much it's worth to you, and what sacrifices you might make in other parts of your life, in order to support those who grow your food. It's also possible to improve food purchasing without increased expense, by avoiding processed and pre-prepared foods, shopping at farmers' markets, and even growing some of your own. By re-evaluating their diets and planning carefully, many people have already disproven the myth that a healthy, sustainable diet must be more expensive.

SUPPORT community-based and worker-run collectives if you need to hire day laborers for yard work, construction, or other projects. Such organizations promote fair and safe employment, improved health, and overall empowerment of migrant workers.

LEARN about issues related to immigration and labor, continuing to educate yourself so that you are prepared to cast a well-informed vote when such items appear on the ballot. Stay informed about legislation affecting those who grow our food and manufacture our goods, and take the opportunity to call up your representatives and influence their votes on such legislation.

Endnotes

Introduction

 1. Migration Dialogue, "Immigration, Naturalization, and Dual Citizen-
    ship," *Migration News* (University of California, Davis), February 1997,
    http://migration.ucdavis.edu/mn/more.php?id=1150_0_2_0-16k.

Chapter 1

 1. The Immigration Reform and Control Act of 1986 granted amnesty to
    millions of migrants already in the U.S., while also tightening border
    security and establishing penalties for employers who hired undocu-
    mented workers.
 2. Eric Holt-Giménez, executive director of Food First and the leader of our
    trip.
 3. Created in response to a labor shortage during World War II and operat-
    ing into the 1960s, the Bracero Program brought a total of more than
    four million temporary seasonal farmworkers from Mexico to the United
    States.
 4. Despite opposition from hundreds of border residents and the cities of
    El Paso, Ciudad Juárez, and Sunland Park, the ASARCO smelter was
    granted a new five-year air quality permit in February 2008 by the Texas
    Commission on Environmental Quality. For more information, see the
    City of El Paso website: http://www.ci.el-paso-tx.us/asarco.asp.
 5. Maquiladoras are foreign-owned factories located in Mexico (usually

near the border), which import machinery and parts for cheap assembly and then reexport the finished product to the U.S.

6. For more information about successful labor practices in California Agriculture, see Ron Strochlic and Kari Hamerschlag, "Best Labor Management Practices on Twelve California Farms: Toward a More Sustainable Food System" (Davis, CA: California Institute for Rural Studies, 2006), http://www.cirsinc.org/Documents/Pub0106.1.pdf.

7. Textile and apparel products were originally governed by special trade restrictions, but with NAFTA, an unlimited quantity of such goods can be imported from Mexico tax free. This made it profitable for companies to relocate their manufacturing south of the border, and the number of textile and apparel maquiladoras increased dramatically.

8. There is actually a significant and constantly growing body of academic research confirming the success of this development model in many places around the world. Angus Wright, personal correspondence, August 2008.

Chapter 2

1. Not to be confused with the Mexican War of Independence ninety years earlier, the Mexican Revolution of 1910 was a popular uprising against the thirty-one-year rule of dictator Porfirio Díaz. One aspect of the revolution was a peasant revolt led by Pancho Villa in Chihuahua and Emiliano Zapata in southern Mexico, demanding redistribution of land to indigenous people and small farmers.

2. Imports can be blocked via quotas (a limit on the number of goods allowed into the country) or by tariffs (taxes on imported goods, to make them more expensive than domestic ones). These are common ways that governments protect their own producers from foreign competition.

3. The World Bank and International Monetary Fund (IMF) are the world's largest public lenders, providing loans to countries of the Global South for debt relief and development projects (such as highways, power plants, irrigation, and schools). These twin organizations were established in 1945 and are collectively owned by the governments of over 180 countries, with the largest and most influential shareholders being the U.S., Japan, Germany, the U.K., and France. To receive loans from the World Bank or IMF, governments must often agree to "structural adjustment programs," which involve cutting public spending, privatizing natural resources, and reducing trade barriers (with the idea that such policies create economic growth so the country can pay back its loans in the future). The debate over the effectiveness of these institutions, and their approach to reducing poverty, is highly contentious and polarized.

4. The General Agreement on Tariffs and Trade (GATT) was a treaty signed by twenty-three countries in 1948, to reduce barriers to international trade. Over the next few decades, GATT grew into a large multilateral

agreement, regulating trade among more than one hundred countries. Agriculture was originally exempt from the agreement, but was later included during the "Uruguay Round" of trade negotiations from 1986 to 1993. That round of negotiations also marked the beginning of the World Trade Organization (WTO), which basically took the place of GATT in shaping and enforcing global trade agreements.

5. While these numbers may not be statistically exact, they serve to illustrate the concept.

6. This is particularly ironic when farmers who have taken loans for the season's fuel and fertilizer must sell their entire crop immediately to pay that debt, and then are themselves forced to purchase corn at the higher price.

7. Farmers will only keep their grain off the market if there's a government program that buys it from them and manages the whole system, as described above, or if they are organized as a cooperative and collectively agree to release only a certain amount of grain per year, in order to keep the price up.

8. Ejidos are communally managed lands established under the Mexican constitution of 1917.

9. Private contracting of ejido land takes place mostly in northwestern agricultural states such as Sinaloa, where people migrate and rent out their land to large industrial-scale farms that grow for export to the U.S.

10. GDP (gross domestic product) is the total value of all goods and services produced within a country and is commonly used as a measure of the national economy.

11. Most hybrid corn seeds cannot be saved and replanted, so they must be purchased new every year.

Chapter 3

1. In the words of rural development specialist Dr. Peter Rosset, "If the people of a country must depend for their next meal on the vagaries of the global economy, on the goodwill of a superpower not to use food as a weapon, or on the unpredictability and high cost of long-distance shipping, that country is not secure in the sense of either national security or food security." Peter Rosset, *Food Sovereignty: Global Rallying Cry of Farmer Movements* (Oakland, CA: Food First, 2003).

2. The term *peasants*, when used to describe the members of La Vía Campesina, includes not only small farmers but also rural landless workers, indigenous groups, pastoralists, and fishing communities.

3. This is a program of the Center for International Policy (CIP), a nonprofit that promotes U.S. foreign policy based on international cooperation and respect for basic human rights. The Americas Policy Program employs a network of writers throughout Latin America, who release publications to inform citizens about key issues related to trade, global-

ization, and development in the Americas. For more information, see the Americas Policy Program website: http://americas.irc-online.org.

4. A Diputado Federal is nearly the equivalent of a congressperson in the U.S. House of Representatives.

5. It is important to note that highly mechanized, commercial corn operations do exist in Mexico, particularly in northern states where a few producers have access to large tracts of land, irrigation, credit, and influence over national policy. Under NAFTA, some of these producers have followed economists' predictions and switched to horticultural crops for export, while some have continued to successfully produce and sell corn. In both cases, the skewed distribution of investment, resources and power in Mexican agriculture has allowed a small minority to thrive while the majority of producers suffer acute marginalization and neglect. Angus Wright, personal communication, August 2008.

6. To learn more about this program, see Jonathan A. Fox and Xochitl Bada, "Migrant Organization and Hometown Impacts in Rural Mexico," *Journal of Agrarian Change* 8, no. 2–3 (May 2008).

Chapter 4

1. The Mexican Friends Service Committee is a Quaker service organization based out of the Casa de los Amigos in Mexico City.

2. For a comprehensive account of this history, see Eric Holt-Giménez, *Campesino a Campesino: Voices from Latin America's Farmer to Farmer Movement for Sustainable Agriculture* (Oakland, CA: Food First, 2006).

3. Cover crops are plants grown for the purpose of being plowed back into the soil to add organic matter, which improves soil structure and fertility. Plants from the legume family are often used as cover crops because they can take nitrogen (an important plant nutrient) from the air and convert it into a form that's available to plants. Cover cropping is a common method of fertilizing the soil in organic farming systems.

4. Integrated pest management is an approach that seeks to reduce or eliminate pesticide use, relying instead on careful monitoring, knowledge of pest life cycles, threshold populations, and the use of organic and biological controls.

5. The "center of origin" of a crop is the place where it was first domesticated (i.e., bred from a wild plant) and therefore the place where the greatest diversity and the plant's wild relatives are to be found. These varieties contain many genetic traits, such as resistance to diseases and pests, that are important to conserve.

6. The Campesino a Campesino Movement in Mexico is fortunate to have developed without oppression by the government. In Guatemala during the 1980s, many farmers were killed or forced to flee the country due to their involvement with the fledgling Campesino a Campesino Movement.

Chapter 5

1. It is important to note that there have been significant efforts in Mexico to train bilingual teachers and develop curriculum in indigenous languages, but such changes are still underway and may not have reached Guelatao. Angus Wright, personal correspondence, August 2008.

2. The Zapatistas are a revolutionary group in Chiapas (the state just south of Oaxaca) fighting for indigenous rights and for local control over their region's natural resources. In 1996, the Mexican government and the Zapatistas signed the San Andrés Accords, in which the government agreed to recognize indigenous communities in the constitution, increase their political representation, promote indigenous culture, guarantee access to basic needs and education, and ensure the legal rights of indigenous peoples to govern themselves. However, the government failed to actually implement these changes, and instead heightened its military presence in Chiapas. See Global Exchange, "The History and Importance of the San Andrés Accords," http://www.globalexchange.org/countries/americas/mexico/SanAndres.html.

3. Amnesty International (AI) sent a delegation to Oaxaca in 2007 to address human rights abuses (police brutality, deaths, arbitrary arrest, torture, and denial of a fair trial) related to the social uprising of the previous year. AI called on both the federal and state governments to investigate all cases of human rights violations, provide fair trials for those detained, and ensure that human rights defenders and journalists could work without threat or harassment. However, AI Secretary General Irene Khan reported that the meeting with the state authorities "was disappointing," and that "the Governor and his colleagues refuse to recognise that serious human rights violations have taken place." Amnesty International, "Mexico: Ensuring justice, the only way forward in Oaxaca," press release, August 1, 2007, http://archive.amnesty.org/library/Index/ENGAMR410432007?open&of=ENG-2AM.

4. At first, the program only allowed strict "hands-off" forest conservation, with no type of active land management or sustainable use. But later, due to ongoing resistance from rural activist groups, it was altered to allow the improvement of existing agroforestry systems (though not the creation of new ones) as a payment-eligible activity, despite pressure from the World Bank to focus only on untouched forests and to exclude agroecosystems such as shade-grown coffee. In a 2004 manifesto, campesino organizations from Mexico and Central America denounced the Payment for Environmental Services approach, saying, "You will not conserve nature by depopulating the countryside, because ecosystems are socially reproduced. To restore lost resources and equilibrium, what is missing is the restoration of a sustainable rural economy, capable of use without destruction." Kathleen McAfee and Elizabeth N. Shapiro, "Payment for Environmental Services in Mexico: Neoliberalism, Social Move-

ments, and the State," paper draft, http://www.allacademic.com//meta/
p_mla_apa_research_citation/2/5/3/7/9/pages253799/p253799-1.php.

5. In April 2008, Jesus León Santos was one of six recipients of the presti-
gious Goldman Environmental Prize (the world's largest prize honoring
grassroots environmentalists), for his work with CEDICAM to restore
highly degraded landscapes in the Mixteca. For more information, see
the Goldman Environmental Prize, North America, 2008, http://www.
goldmanprize.org/2008/northamerica.

6. This is an oversimplification of Mixtec history, in which an elite noble
class controlled the fertile bottomlands, while the lower classes eked out
a living on the steep surrounding hills and mountains. In fact, as soil
eroded these slopes and accumulated in the valleys, the nobility forced
lower-class laborers to build dams to capture the runoff, and, gradually, a
system of fertile terraces evolved. So it was actually the deforestation and
land degradation of the slopes *prior* to the arrival of the Spaniards that
drove impoverished indigenous farmers ever higher into the mountains,
while allowing agriculture in the valleys to flourish. For a more detailed
description of the impacts of Spanish colonization on the Mixtec people,
and on pre- and postcolonial Mexican agriculture in general, see Angus
Wright, *The Death of Ramón González* (Austin, TX: UT Press, 2005).

Epilogue

1. Martin Khor, "U.S. Farm Bill is a 'Setback' for Doha Negotiations,"
SUNS—South-North Development Monitor, August 16, 2007, http://www.
twnside.org.sg/title2/wto.info/twninfo080704.htm. Farm Policy.com: A
Summary of Farm Policy News, "The New Farm Bill and WTO Litigation
Concerns," August 6, 2008, http://www.farmpolicy.com/?p=855. USDA
Foreign Agriculture Service, *Fact Sheet: North American Free Trade Agree*
ment, January 2008, http://www.fas.usda.gov/info/factsheets/NAFTA.asp.
James Auger, "NAFTA Members Complete Agricultural Liberalisation
Process, Mexican Farmers Protest" *Global Insight*, January 4, 2008, www.
thailandwto.org/Doc/News/5735.pdf. Agence France-Presse, "Farmers
Clog Mexico City in Corn Tariff Protest," January 31, 2008, http://afp.
google.com/article/ALeqM5hDUCfa3JCjUuDZcRUdkTGGP3dRvg.

2. Agence France-Presse, "Farmers Clog Mexico City in Corn Tariff Protest."
Marla Dickerson, "NAFTA has its trade-offs for the U.S.," *Los Angeles
Times*, March 3, 2008, sec. A-1, http://articles.latimes.com/2008/mar/03/
business/fi-nafta3. GovTrack.us, *H.R. 4329—110th Congress (2007):
NAFTA Accountability Act*. 2007, August 6, 2008, http://www.govtrack.us/
congress/bill.xpd?tab=summary&bill=h110-4329. Library of Congress,
THOMAS. *H.R. 4329: NAFTA Accountability Act*, 2007, http://thomas.loc.
gov/cgi-bin/query/z?c110:H.R.4329.IH:.

3. The Department of Homeland Security, *Southwest Border Fence*, August

13, 2008, http://www.dhs.gov/xprevprot/programs/border-fence-south-west.shtm. Border Trade Alliance, "Impacts of DHS Presidential Transition On Borders Uncertain," BTA Border blog, July 29, 2008, http://www.thebta.org/content/2008/07/29/impacts-of-dhs-presidential-transition-on-borders-uncertain/.

4. Dianne Solís and Stella M. Chávez, "Illegal immigrants returning home in large numbers," *Dallas Morning News*, July 31, 2008, http://www.dallasnews.com/sharedcontent/dws/news/localnews/stories/DN-exodus_31met.ART.State.Edition2.4d7274b.html. Steven A. Camarota and Karen Jensenius, "Homeward Bound: Recent Immigration Enforcement and the Decline in the Illegal Alien Population," Center for Immigration Studies, Backgrounders and Reports, July 2008, http://www.cis.org/trends_and_enforcement. Tabitha Holland, "Report Finds Decline in Number of US Illegal Immigrants," Global Visas.com, July 31, 2008, http://www.globalvisas.com/news/report_finds_decline_in_number_of_us_illegal_immigrants347.html. Mike Swift, "Is U.S. losing its appeal for illegal immigrants?" *San Jose Mercury News*, July 31, 2008, http://www.mercurynews.com/ci_10052763.

5. Jakarta, "An Answer to the Global Food Crisis: Peasants and Small Farmers Can Feed the World!" La Vía Campesina, April 24, 2008, http://viacampesina.org/main_en/index.php?option=com_content&task=view&id=525&Itemid=1. Walden Bello, "Manufacturing a Food Crisis," *Nation*, June 2, 2008, http://www.thenation.com/doc/20080602/bello. Vivienne Walt, "The World's Growing Food-Price Crisis," *TIME*, February 27, 2008, http://www.time.com/time/world/article/0,8599,1717572,00.html. Stephen Lendman, "Global Food Crisis: Hunger Plagues Haiti and the World," *Global Research* (Center for Research on Globalization), April 21, 2008, http://www.globalresearch.ca/index.php?context=va&aid=8754.

6. Bello, "Manufacturing a Food Crisis." Laura Carlsen, "Behind Latin America's Food Crisis," Hungry for Justice: How the World Food System Fails the Poor (#11), America's Policy Program Special Report (Interhemispheric Center for International Policy), May 19, 2008, http://americas.irc-online.org/am/5236. Matthew Little, "Food Prices Skyrocket Amidst Growing Shortages," *Epoch Times*, April 11, 2008, http://en.epochtimes.com/news/8-4-11/68956.html.

7. Jakarta, "An Answer to the Global Food Crisis." Bello, "Manufacturing a Food Crisis." Walt, "The World's Growing Food-Price Crisis." Lendman, "Global Food Crisis." Carlsen, "Behind Latin America's Food Crisis."

8. Carlsen, "Behind Latin America's Food Crisis." Jo Tuckman, "Mexico Freezes Food Prices in Response to Global Crisis," *Guardian*, June 20, 2008, http://www.guardian.co.uk/world/2008/jun/20/mexico.food?gusrc=rss&feed=worldnews. Daniel Hernandez, "Confronting Food

Shortages in Mexico," *LA Daily*, June 3, 2008, http://blogs.laweekly.com/
ladaily/letter-from-mexico-city/confronting-food-shortages-in/. *Prensa
Latina*, "Transnats Capitalize on Food Crisis," June 12, 2008, http://www.
plenglish.com.mx/article.asp?ID=%7B22C5BAA7-7FDC-434F-B73F-FDA
45569638D%7D)&language=EN. Diego Cevallos, "MEXICO: Latest
Measures Against Food Crisis Called Ineffective," Inter Press Service News
Agency, June 19, 2008, http://ipsnews.net/news.asp?idnews=42890.

9. Carlsen, "Behind Latin America's Food Crisis." Food and Agriculture
Organization, United Nations, "High Level Conference on World Food
Security: The Challenges of Climate Change and Bioenergy," Rome, June
3–5, 2008, http://www.fao.org/foodclimate/hlc-home/en/. Richard
Owen, "UN Food Summit Hammers Out Plan for World's Hungry,"
Times Online, June 4, 2008, http://www.timesonline.co.uk/tol/news/
world/article4064650.ece. FAO Newsroom, "Food Summit Calls for More
Investment in Agriculture," June 6, 2008, http://www.fao.org/newsroom/
en/news/2008/1000856/index.html. Timothy Charles Holmseth, "UN
Reviews Impact of Biofuels on Food Sector," *Ethanol Producer Magazine*,
August 2008, http://ethanolproducer.com/article-print.jsp?article_id=
4429. La Vía Campesina, "The G8 Is Using the Food Crisis to Promote
Their Free Trade Agenda," press release, July 9, 2008, http://www.viacam-
pesina.org/main_en/index.php?option=com_content&task=view&id=57
9&Itemid=38.

10. Jakarta, "An Answer to the Global Food Crisis." Bello, "Manufacturing
a Food Crisis." Carsen, *Hungry for Justice*. Agence France-Presse, "Small
Farmers Slam 'Empty Policies' Ahead of FAO Food Summit," June 1,
2008, http://afp.google.com/article/ALeqM5jFGOdTX-P_l0hBLR8SMn
Z8Pjpy9Q.

11. Abate Tsedeke, et al., *Executive Summary of the Synthesis Report*, International Assessment of Agricultural Knowledge, Science and Technology
for Development (IAASTD), April 2008, http://www.agassessment.org/
docs/SR_Exec_Sum_280508_English.pdf. BioScienceResource.org,
"How the Science Media Failed the IAASTD," BioScience Resource Project Commentaries (BioScience Resource), April 7, 2008, http://www.
bioscienceresource.org/commentaries/brc9Howthesciencemediafailed
theIAASTD.php.

12. BioScienceResource.org, "How the Science Media Failed the IAASTD."
Stephen Leahy, "Towards a New and Improved Green Revolution," Inter
Press Service News Agency, April 6, 2008, http://ipsnews.net/news.asp?
idnews=41877. Ana de Ita, *Fourteen Years of NAFTA and the Tortilla Crisis*,
Interhemispheric Resources Center Americas Program, January 10, 2008,
http://americas.irc-online.org/am/4879. Editorial, "Deserting the hungry?" *Nature* 451 (2008), 223–24. Editorial, "Off the rails," *Nature Biotechnology* 26 (2008), 247. Erik Stokstad, "Dueling Visions for a Hungry

World," *Science* 319 (2008), 1474–76. John Vidal, "Change in Farming Can Feed the World—report," *Guardian*, April 16, 2008, http://www. guardian.co.uk/environment/2008/apr/16/food.biofuels. Ben Block, "International Commission Calls for 'Paradigm Shift' in Agriculture," *Worldwatch Institute News*, April 18, 2008, http://www.worldwatch.org/ node/5712.

References for Background Boxes

Conditions for U.S. Farmworkers

The Agricultural Justice Project. *The Agricultural Justice Project: For All Who Labor in Agriculture.* 2007. http://www.cata-farmworkers.org/ajp/index.html.

Coalition of Immokalee Workers. "Facts and Figures on Farmworkers and the Agricultural Industry: Farmworker Poverty and Agriculture Industry Economics." CIW Online Headquarters, 2008. http://www.ciw-online.org/8-stats.html.

Farmworker Justice. "Farmworkers and Pesticides." 2008. http://www.fwjustice.org/Health&Safety/Pesticides.htm.

Food Alliance. "About Food Alliance." http://www.foodalliance.org/about.

Larson, Alice. "Environment/Occupational Safety and Health." *Migrant Health Issues.* Monograph 2: 6–15. Buda, TX: National Center for Farmworker Health, Inc., October 2001. http://www.ncfh.org/docs/02%20-%20environment.pdf.

Lighthall, David. "The Poor Health of Farmworkers." *Western Journal of Medicine* 175 (2001): 223–24. http://www.pubmedcentral.nih.gov/articlerender.fcgi?artid=1071557.

National Center for Farmworker Health, Inc. "Facts about Farmworkers." Buda, TX. http://www.ncfh.org/docs/fs-Facts%20about%20Farmworkers.pdf.

___. "Overview of America's Farmworkers." 1985–2002: 1-4. http://www.ncfh.org/aaf_01.php.

Oxfam America. *Like Machines in the Fields: Workers Without Rights in Ameri-*

can Agriculture. March 2004. http://www.oxfamamerica.org/newsand
publications/publications/research_reports/art7011.html/OA-Like_
Machines_in_the_Fields.pdf.

Reeves, Margaret, et al. *Fields of Poison 2002: California Farmworkers and Pesticides.* Californians for Pesticide Reform, 2002. http://www.panna.org/
docsWorkers/CPRreport.pdf.

Mills P., and S. Kwong "Cancer Incidence in the United Farmworkers of
America (UFW), 1987–1997." *American Journal of Industrial Medicine* 40
(2001): 596–603.

United Farm Workers of America. "Legislation: CA Heat Regulations." 2008.
http://www.ufw.org/_board.php?mode=view&b_code=cre_leg&b_no=4.

United States Department of Labor. Employment Standards Administration.
Wage and Hour Division. *Fact Sheet #51: Field Sanitation Standards Under the
Occupational Safety and Health Act.* January 2008. http://www.dol.gov/esa/
whd/regs/compliance/whdfs51.pdf.

United States Department of Labor. Employment Standards Administration.
Office of the Assistant Secretary for Policy, Office of Programmatic Policy.
*Findings of the National Agricultural Workers Survey (NAWS) 2001–2002: A
Demographic and Employment Profile of United States Farmworkers.* March
2005. http://www.doleta.gov/agworker/report9/naws_rpt9.pdf.

___. *Findings of the National Agricultural Workers Survey (NAWS) 1997–1998: A
Demographic and Employment Profile of United States Farmworkers.* March
2000. http://www.doleta.gov/agworker/report_9.pdf.

Villarejo, Don, et al. *Access to Health Care for California's Hired Farm Workers:
A Baseline Report.* California Program on Access to Care, California Policy
Research Center, University of California, Berkeley, October 2001.
http://cpac.berkeley.edu/documents/farmworkerhealthcare.pdf.

___, and S.A. McCurdy. "The California Agricultural Workers Health Survey."
Journal of Agricultural Safety and Health 14 (2008): 135–46.

The U.S.-Mexico Border Fence

Ackleson, Jason. "Fencing in Failure: Effective Border Control Is Not
Achieved by Building More Fences." *Immigration Policy in Focus* 4 (April
2005). http://www.immigrationpolicy.org/index.php?content=f050401.

Associated Press. "AP/Ipsos Poll: US Presses to Complete Border Fence, Even
as Americans Are Split on the Idea." April 28, 2008. http://surveys.ap.org/
data/Ipsos/national/2008-03-06%20AP%20Border%20Topline.pdf.

Center for Biological Diversity. "Borderlands and Boundary Waters." 2008.
http://www.biologicaldiversity.org/swcbd/PROGRAMS/blbw/index.html.

Hendricks, Tyche. "On the Border." *San Francisco Chronicle*, sec. A-1, December 2005. http://www.sfgate.com/cgi-bin/article.cgi?file=/c/a/2005/12/03/
MNGHQG2FV91.DTL3.

Hsu, Spencer S., and William Branigin. "Anti-Terrorism Efforts Hailed:

Chertoff Says Security Improvements Thwart Extremists." *Washington Post*, sec. A04, March 7, 2008. http://www.washingtonpost.com/ wp-dyn/content/article/2008/03/06/AR2008030601435.html.

CTV.ca News. "Mexico urges Canada to help oppose border fence." October 26, 2006. http://www.ctv.ca/servlet/ArticleNews/story/CTVNews/ 20061026/mexico_fence_061026/20061026?hub=TopStories.

No Border Wall. 2007. http://www.notexasborderwall.com.

Nuñez-Neto, Blas, and Yule Kim. *Border Security: Barriers Along the U.S. International Border*. CRS Report for Congress, Congress Research Service, May 13, 2008. http://fpc.state.gov/documents/organization/105162.pdf.

Pomfret, John. "As Border Crackdown Intensifies, a Tribe Is Caught in the Crossfire." *Washington Post*, sec. A1, September 15, 2006. http://www. washingtonpost.com/wdyn/content/article/2006/09/14/AR2006091401827.html.

Segee, Brian P., and Jenny L. Neeley. Defenders of Wildlife. *On the Line: The Impacts of Immigration Policy on Wildlife and Habitat in the Arizona Borderlands*. 2006. http://www.defenders.org/programs_and_policy/habitat_conservation/federal_lands/border_policy/.

United States General Accounting Office. *Overstay Tracking: A Key Component of Homeland Security and a Layered Defense*. May 2004. www.gao.gov/ highlights/d0482high.pdf.

U.S. Department of Homeland Security, U.S. Customs and Border Protection, and U.S. Border Patrol. *Environmental Stewardship Plan for the Construction, Operation, and Maintenance of Tactical Infrastructure, Rio Grande Valley Sector, Texas*. July 2008. http://www.borderfenceplanning.com/wp-content/ uploads/2008/07/pf225-rgv-esp.pdf.

NAFTA and the U.S.-Mexico Border

American Friends Service Committee. "NAFTA—and Beyond." *Mexico-U.S. Border: Working for Justice in the Maquiladora Industry*. 2008. http://www. afsc.org/mexico-us-border/naftaandbeyond.htm.

Audley, John J., et al. *NAFTA's Promise and Reality: Lessons from Mexico for the Hemisphere*. Carnegie Endowment for International Peace, November 2003. http://www.carnegieendowment.org/files/nafta1.pdf.

Auger, James. "NAFTA Members Complete Agricultural Liberalisation Process, Mexican Farmers Protest." Global Insight, January 4, 2008. www.thailandwto.org/Doc/News/5735.pdf.

Brown, Garrett D. *NAFTA's 10 Year Failure to Protect Mexican Workers' Health and Safety*. Maquiladora Health and Safety Support Network, December 2004. http://mhssn.igc.org/NAFTA_2004.pdf.

Brown, Timothy C. "The Fourth Member of NAFTA: The U.S.-Mexico Border." *The Annals of the American Academy of Political and Social Science. NAFTA Revisited: Expectations and Realities* 550 (1997): 105–29.

Gallagher, Kevin P. "Is NAFTA Working for Mexico?" *The Environmental Forum*

(May/June 2006). Tufts University. http://ase.tufts.edu/gdae/Pubs/rp/
EnvForumNAFTAMay06.pdf.

Griswold, Daniel T. "NAFTA at 10: An Economic and Foreign Policy Success."
Center for Trade Policy Studies, Cato Institute. *Free Trade Bulletin* 1
(December 2002). http://www.freetrade.org/pubs/FTBs/FTB-001.pdf.

Office of the United States Trade Representative. *NAFTA Facts: NAFTA Myths
vs. Facts.* March 2008. http://www.ustr.gov/assets/Document_Library/
Fact_Sheets/2008/asset_upload_file855_14540.pdf.

Reuters. "Mexican president defends NAFTA despite protests." January 7,
2008. http://www.reuters.com/article/worldNews/idUSN07621613200
80107.

Scott, Robert E. "The High Price of 'Free' Trade: NAFTA's Failure Has Cost the
United States Jobs Across the Nation." Briefing Paper #147, Economic
Policy Institute, November 2003. http://www.epi.org/content.cfm/
briefingpapers_bp147.

___, et al. "Revisiting NAFTA: Still Not Working for North America's
Workers." Briefing Paper #173, Economic Policy Institute, September
2006. http://www.epi.org/content.cfm/bp173.

Shapleigh, Eliot, Wesley Leonard and Cynthia Conroy. "The Environmental
Economic Consequences of Border Industrialization in the NAFTA Era."
In *Texas Borderlands: Frontier of the Future.* 4th ed. Center for Environmental Resource Management, University of Texas at El Paso, 2007.
http://www.shapleigh.org/system/reporting_document/file/178/9_
environment_chapter.pdf.

Stiglitz, Joseph E., and Andrew Charlton. *Fair Trade for All: How Trade Can
Promote Development.* New York: Oxford University Press, 2005.

Maquiladoras

Arriola, Elvia R. *Accountability for Murder in the Maquiladoras: Linking Corporate
Indifference to Gender Violence at the U.S.-Mexico Border.* Women on the Border, 2007. http://www.womenontheborder.org/accountability_murders.
htm.

Bacon, David. *The Children of NAFTA: Labor Wars on the U.S./Mexico Border.*
Berkeley: University of California Press, 2004.

___. Interview with Julia Quiñones. "Hunger on the Border." *David Bacon:
Photographs and Stories; Mexico.* January 25, 2006. http://dbacon.igc.org/
Mexico/2006hunger.html.

Brown, Garrett D. *NAFTA's 10 Year Failure to Protect Mexican Workers' Health
and Safety.* Maquiladora Health and Safety Support Network. December
2004. http://mhssn.igc.org/NAFTA_2004.pdf.

Contreras, Oscar F. "Industrial Development and Technology Policy: The
Case of the Maquiladoras." *The Changing Structure of Mexico: Political Social
and Economic Prospects.* 2nd ed. Edited by Laura Randall. Armonk: M.E.
Sharpe, 2006. 267–77.

CorpWatch: Holding Corporations Accountable. "Maquiladoras at a Glance."
    July 30, 1999. http://www.corpwatch.org/article.php?id=1528#map5.

Galindo, Alma Leticia Puente, et al. Comité Fronterizo de Obreros (CFO).
    "Justicia! The Ethical Clothing Lsabel and the Maquiladora Dignidad y
    Justicia." http://www.cfomaquiladoras.org/english%20site/about_
    dignidad_yjusticia.en.html#top.

Hendricks, Tyche. "On the Border: Maquiladoras," *San Francisco Chronicle*,
    November 27, 2005.

Hernández, Martín Amaru Barrios. "Maquilatitlán: City of Indians becomes
    Jean Capital of Mexico." Maquiladora Solidarity Network, March 1, 2004.
    http://en.maquilasolidarity.org/en/node/452.

Huato, Julio. "Maquiladoras and Standard of Living in Mexico Before
    and After NAFTA." Diss., City University of New York, May 22, 2005.
    http://129.3.20.41/econ-wp/dev/papers/0508/0508006.pdf.

Interfaith Center for Corporate Responsibility. "Landmark Study Shows
    Mexican Maquiladora Workers Not Able to Meet Basic Needs on Sweat-
    shop Wages." Press release. June 28, 2001. http://www.iccr.org/news/
    press_releases/2001/pr_maquila.htm.

Kamel, Rachael, and Anya Hoffman. *The Maquiladora Reader: Cross-Border
    Organizing Since NAFTA.* n.p.: American Friends Service Committee, 1999.

Made in Mexico, Inc: Maquiladora Management Services. "Discover the Cost-
    Saving Benefits of Mexico Manufacturing with Maquiladoras." 1996–2008.
    http://www.madeinmexicoinc.com.

Noruega: El portal oficial en México. "Business in Mexico: Maquiladora."
    2007. http://www.noruega.org.mx/Business_eng/sector/Maquiladora/
    maquiladora.htm.

Sandoval, Daniel. "Maquiladora: Along the Mexico-US Border, Past, Present,
    and Future." June 5, 2003. Unpublished ms. for EDGE: Poverty and Global
    Development, Stanford University. http://www.stanford.edu/class/e297c/
    Maquiladora%20along%20the%20Mexico-US%20Border.pdf

Winn, Peter. *Americas: The Changing Face of Latin America and the Caribbean.*
    Berkeley: University of California Press, 1999.

Origins of the Green Revolution in Mexico

Barry, Tom. *Zapata's Revenge: Free Trade and the Farm Crisis in Mexico.* Boston:
    Interhemispheric Resource Center, 1995.

Federal Research Division, Library of Congress. "Government Agricultural
    Policy." In *Mexico: A Country Study.* Edited by Tim L. Merrill and Ramón
    Miró. June 1996. http://www.country-data.com/cgi-bin/query/
    r-8743.html.

Hewitt de Alcántara, Cynthia. *Modernizing Mexican Agriculture: Socioeconomic
    Implications of Technological Change 1940-1970.* Geneva: United Nations
    Research Institute for Social Development, 1976.

Jennings, Bruce H. *Foundations of International Agricultural Research: Sciences
    and Politics in Mexican Agriculture.* Boulder: Westview Press, 1988.

Wright, Angus. *The Death of Ramón González: The Modern Agricultural Dilemma.* 2nd ed. Austin: University of Texas Press, 2005.

Biofuels in Mexico

Chavez, Luis, and Jeff Nawn. *Mexico Bio-Fuels Annual Report 2007.* USDA Foreign Agricultural Service GAIN Report, no. MX7042, June 12, 2007. http://www.fas.usda.gov/gainfiles/200706/146291366.pdf.

Holt-Giménez, Eric. *Biofuels: Myths of the Agrofuels Transition.* Food First/ Institute for Food and Development Policy, July 6, 2007. http://www. foodfirst.org/en/node/1712.

___. *U.S. Biofuels eating into Mexican Tortillas?* Food First/Institute for Food and Development Policy, January 18, 2007. http://www.foodfirst.org/en/ node/1604.

Millard, Peter. "Mexico President Calderón Cautious on Using Food for Biofuels." *Dow Jones Newswires,* May 19, 2008. http://www.cattlenetwork. com/Grain_Content.asp?ContentID=222775.

Pimentel, David, and Tad W. Patzek. "Ethanol Production Using Corn, Switchgrass, and Wood; Biodiesel Production Using Soybean and Sun-flower." *Natural Resources Research* 14 (2005): 65–76. http://petroleum. berkeley.edu/papers/Biofuels/NRRethanol.2005.pdf.

Quiroz, Sitna. "Biofuels, Corn Prices and Food Security in Mexico." On *Latin America and the Caribbean Blog at ODI* (Overseas Development Institute) website, March 27, 2007. http://lac.civiblog.org/blog/_archives/2007/3/ 27/2838904.html.

Wiessner, Christian. "Hard for poor nations to hike food output: Mexico." Reuters, May 19, 2008. http://www.reuters.com/article/gc08/idUSN1916 685620080519.

___. "Mexico to issue permits for biofuel production." Reuters UK, February 4, 2008. http://uk.reuters.com/article/environmentNews/idUKN0459613 820080204.

World Energy: Biofuels Leadership in Action. "News of the Day," January 7, 2008. http://www.worldenergy.net/public_information/show_news. php?nid=181. [Calderon quote.]

Agricultural Guest-Worker Programs

Bruno, Andorra. *Immigration: Policy Considerations Related to Guest Worker Programs.* Congressional Research Service, Library of Congress, January 17, 2008. http://italy.usembassy.gov/pdf/other/RL32044.pdf.

DerVartanian, Adrienne. "Renewed Push for AgJOBS." *Farmworker Justice News* 22 (Fall 2007).

Levine, Linda. *The Effects on U.S. Farm Workers of an Agricultural Guest Worker Program.* Congressional Research Service, Library of Congress, March 9, 2006. http://leahy.senate.gov/issues/Immigration/GuestWorker.pdf.

Marentes, Carlos. "Los Braceros: 1942–1964," *The Farmworkers' Website,*1997. http://www.farmworkers.org/benglish.html.

Morgan, Larry C., and Bruce L. Gardner. "Potential for a U.S. Guest-Worker Program in Agriculture: Lessons from the Braceros." *The Gateway: U.S. Immigration Issues and Policies*. Edited by Barry Chiswick. Washington: American Enterprise Institute, 1982.

Winn, Peter. *Americas: The Changing Face of Latin America and the Caribbean*. 3rd ed. Berkeley: University of California Press, 2007.

Wise, Donald E. "The Effect of the Bracero on Agricultural Production in California." *Economic Inquiry* 12 (December 1974): 547–58.

Government Support for Agriculture in Mexico

Barry, Tom. *Zapata's Revenge: Free Trade and the Farm Crisis in Mexico*. Boston: Interhemispheric Resource Center, 1995.

Bethell, Leslie. *Latin America since 1930: Mexico, Central America and the Caribbean*. Cambridge University Press, 1990. Vol. 7 of *Cambridge History of Latin America*.

Federal Research Division, Library of Congress. "Government Agricultural Policy." In *Mexico: A Country Study*. Edited by Tim L. Merrill and Ramón Miró. June 1996. http://www.country-data.com/cgi-bin/query/r-8743. html.

Henriques, Gisele, and Raj Patel. *NAFTA, Corn, and Mexico's Agricultural Trade Liberalization*. IRC Americas Program Special Report, Interhemispheric Resources Center Americas Program, January 28, 2004. http://www. americaspolicy.org/reports/2004/0402nafta.html.

Holt-Giménez, Eric. "Chilpancingo Declaration for Food Sovereignty in Mexico Issued 1-26-2007." Food First/Institute for Food and Development Policy, February 23, 2007. http://www.foodfirst.org/en/node/1650.

Jacinto, Martin. *Calderón, NAFTA, and Mexico's Campesinos in 2008*. Council on Hemispheric Affairs, April 1, 2008. http://www.coha.org/2008/04/calderon-nafta-and-mexico%e2%80%99s-campesinos-in-2008/.

Raat, W. Dirk, and Willam H. Beezley. *Twentieth-century Mexico*. Lincoln: University of Nebraska Press, 1986.

Suppan, Steve. "Mexican Corn, NAFTA, and Hunger," Food Security Fact Sheet No. 3, Institute for Agriculture and Trade Policy, May 1996. http://www.iatp.org/iatp/publications.cfm?accountID=451&refID=23720.

Volker, Hamann. "The Impact of NAFTA on Agricultural Development in Mexico." Conference on International Agricultural Research for Development, Deutscher Tropentag, Witzenhausen, October 9–11, 2002. http://www.tropentag.de/2002/abstracts/full/45.pdf.

Yunez-Naude, Antonio. "The Dismantling of CONASUPO, a Mexican State Trader in Agriculture". *The World Economy* 26 (January 2003): 97–122. http://ssrn.com/abstract=514024.

Direct Marketing in Agriculture

Ahern, Jim, and Marianne M. Wolf. "California Farmers' Markets Seller Price

Perceptions: The Normative and the Positive." *Journal of Food Distribution Research* (March 2002): 20–24. http://ageconsearch.umn.edu/bitstream/27640/1/33010020.pdf.

Holt-Giménez, Eric, et al. *Fair to the Last Drop: The Corporate Challenges to Fair Trade Coffee*. Food First/Institute for Food and Development Policy, October 2007. http://www.foodfirst.org/node/1794.

James, Deborah. "Justice and Java: Coffee in a Fair Trade Market." Global Exchange, September/October 2000. http://www.globalexchange.org/campaigns/fairtrade/coffee/nacla1000.html.

National Conference of State Legislatures. *Access to Healthy Food: Direct Marketing*. March 2005. http://www.ncsl.org/programs/health/publichealth/foodaccess/directmarketing.htm.

Stewart, Hayden. "How Low Has the Farm Share of Retail Food Prices Really Fallen?" *Economic Research Report Number 24*, United States Department of Agriculture, Economic Research Service, August 2006. http://www.ers.usda.gov/publications/err24/err24.pdf.

United Nations Food and Agriculture Organization. *State of Food Insecurity in the World*. 2004. ftp://ftp.fao.org/docrep/fao/007/y5650e/y5650e00.pdf.

United States Department of Agriculture. "Profiling Food Consumption in America." Chapter 2 of *Agriculture Factbook 2001–2002*. http://www.usda.gov/factbook/chapter2.htm#costoffood.

United States Department of Agriculture. Economic Research Service. *Data Sets: Price Spreads from Farmer to Consumer*. May 28, 2008. http://www.ers.usda.gov/Data/FarmToConsumer/Data/marketingbilltable1.htm.

United States Department of Agriculture. National Agricultural Statistics Service. "Farm Resources, Income, and Expenses." Chapter 9 of *2007 Agricultural Statistics*. August 28, 2008. http://www.nass.usda.gov/Publications/Ag_Statistics/2007/CHAP09.PDF.

Wiseman, Tim. "Despite Rising Food Prices, Farmers' Share of Food Dollar Still Falling." *Institute for Rural Journalism and Community Issues blog*, March 27, 2008. http://irjci.blogspot.com/2008/03/despite-rising-food-prices-farmers.html.

Effects of Synthetic Fertilizers on Soil

Altieri, Miguel. *Genetic Engineering in Agriculture: The Myths, Environmental Risks, and Alternatives*. 2nd ed. Oakland, CA: Food First Books, 2004.

Badgley, Catherine, et al. "Organic Agriculture and the Global Food Supply." *Renewable Agriculture and Food Systems* 22 (2007): 86–108. http://journals.cambridge.org/action/displayAbstract?fromPage=online&aid=1091304.

Kramer, Sasha, et al. "Reduced Nitrate Leaching and Enhanced Denitrifier Activity and Efficiency in Organically Fertilized Soils." *Proceedings of the National Academy of Sciences of the United States of America* 103 (March 2006): 4522–27. http://www.pnas.org/cgi/content/full/103/12/4522#B2.

Sullivan, Preston. *Sustainable Soil Management: Soil Systems Guide*. National

Sustainable Agriculture Information Service, May 2004. http://www.attra. ncat.org/attra-pub/PDF/soilmgmt.pdf.

United Nations Food and Agriculture Organization. *International Conference on Organic Agriculture and Food Security Report*, Rome, May 3–5 2007. ftp://ftp.fao.org/paia/organicag/ofs/OFSreport.pdf.

La Vía Campesina: The International Peasant Movement

Desmarais, Annette A. *La Vía Campesina: Globalization and the Power of Peasants*. London: Pluto Press, 2007.

___. *United in the Vía Campesina*. Food First Backgrounder, Food First/Institute for Food and Development Policy, Fall 2005. http://www.foodfirst.org/en/ backgrounders/fall2005.

Food First/Institute for Food and Development Policy. "Global Small-Scale Farmers' Movement Developing New Trade Regimes." *News & Views* 28 (Spring/Summer 2005): 2.

La Vía Campesina: International Peasant Movement website. 2008. http://www.viacampesina.org.

Winfuhr, Michael, and Jennie Jonsén. "Food Sovereignty: Towards Democracy in Localized Food Systems. FIAN-International. London: ITDG Publishing, 2005.

The U.S. Farm Bill

Fanjul, Gonzalo, and Arabella Fraser. Oxfam International. *Dumping without Borders: How U.S. Agricultural Policies Are Destroying the Livelihoods of Mexican Corn Farmers*. August 27, 2003. http://www.mindfully.org/WTO/ 2003/US-Mexican-Oxfam27aug03.htm.

Imhoff, Daniel. *Food Fight: The Citizen's Guide to a Food and Farm Bill*. Healdsburg: Watershed Media, 2007.

Kupfer, Patty, et al. *Reaping the Seeds We Sow: U.S. Farm Policy and the Immigration Dilemma*. Building Sustainable Futures for Farmers Globally, 2007. http://www.globalfarmer.org/Uploads/immigration%20paper2.pdf.

Moberg, David. "Whose Subsidy Is It Anyway? Farmers take the heat, but Big Ag reaps the farm bill benefits." Institute for Agriculture and Trade Policy. *Ag Observatory* (June 4, 2007). http://www.agobservatory.org/headlines. cfm?RefID=98906.

Ray, Daryll E. *Agricultural Policy for the Twenty-First Century and the Legacy of the Wallaces*. Agricultural Policy Analysis Center, Department of Economics, University of Tennessee, 2008.

Spieldoch, Alexandra, and Bill Lilliston. *A Fair Farm Bill and Immigration*. Institute for Agriculture and Trade Policy, July 2007. http://www. agobservatory.org/library.cfm?refid=99390.

United States Department of Agriculture. *Strengthening the Foundation for Future Growth in U.S. Agriculture*. 2007 Farm Bill Theme Paper. September 2006. http://www.usda.gov/documents/Farmbill07foundationssumf.pdf.

NAFTA: Effects on Agriculture

Barry, Tom. *Zapata's Revenge: Free Trade and the Farm Crisis in Mexico.* Boston: Interhemispheric Resource Center, 1995.

Carlsen, Laura. *NAFTA Inequality and Immigration.* Interhemispheric Resources Center Americas Policy Program, October 31, 2007. http://americas. irc-online.org/pdf/reports/0711nafta-eng.pdf.

de Ita, Ana. *Fourteen Years of NAFTA and the Tortilla Crisis.* Interhemispheric Resources Center Americas Program, January 10, 2008. http://americas. irc-online.org/am/4879.

Henriques, Gisele, and Raj Patel. *NAFTA, Corn, and Mexico's Agricultural Trade Liberalization.* IRC Americas Program Special Report, Interhemispheric Resources Center Americas Program, January 28, 2004. http://www. americaspolicy.org/reports/2004/0402nafta.html.

Meléndez Salinas, Claudia. "Mexican Farmers Struggle to Survive: NAFTA, Farm Bill, Lack of Other Economic Opportunities Force Subsistence Producers to Find Work Elsewhere." *Monterey County Herald*, December 5, 2007. http://www.montereyherald.com/ci_7616170.

Scott, Robert E., et al. "Revisiting NAFTA: Still Not Working for North America's Workers." EPI Briefing Paper #173, Economic Policy Institute, September 2006. http://www.epi.org/content.cfm/bp173.

Stiglitz, Joseph E., and Andrew Charlton. *Fair Trade for All: How Trade Can Promote Development.* New York: Oxford University Press, 2005.

United States Department of Agriculture. Foreign Agriculture Service. *North American Free Trade Agreement.* 2008. http://www.fas.usda.gov/itp/Policy/ NAFTA/nafta.asp.

Wright, Angus. *The Death of Ramón González: The Modern Agricultural Dilemma.* 2nd ed. Austin: University of Texas Press, 2005.

Zahniser, Steven, and William Coyle. *U.S.-Mexico Corn Trade During the NAFTA Era: New Twists to an Old Story.* USDA Economic Research Service, May 2004. http://www.ers.usda.gov/publications/FDS/may04/fds04D01/ fds04D01.pdf

The Green Revolution and Peasant Agriculture

Barry, Tom. *Zapata's Revenge: Free Trade and the Farm Crisis in Mexico.* Boston: Interhemispheric Resource Center, 1995.

Clawson, David L., and Don R. Hoy. "Nealtican, Mexico: A Peasant Community That Rejected the 'Green Revolution.'" *American Journal of Economics and Sociology*, 38 (1979): 371–87.

Gliessman, Stephen. R. *Agroecology: The Ecology of Sustainable Food Systems.* 2nd ed. New York: Taylor & Francis Group, 2007.

Hewitt de Alcántara, Cynthia. *Modernizing Mexican Agriculture: Socioeconomic Implications of Technological Change 1940–1970.* Geneva: United Nations Research Institute for Social Development, 1976.

Jennings, Bruce H. *Foundations of International Agricultural Research: Sciences and Politics in Mexican Agriculture.* Boulder: Westview Press, 1988.

Klein-Robbenhaar, John J.I. "Agro-Industry and the Environment: The Case of Mexico in the 1990's." *Agricultural History* 69 (1995): 395–412. http://www.jstor.org/stable/3744335.

Pimentel, D., and Marcia Pimentel. "Comment: Adverse Environmental Consequences of the Green Revolution." *Population and Development Review* 16 (1990): 329–32.

Sonnenfeld, David A. "Mexico's 'Green Revolution,' 1940–1980: Towards an Environmental History." *Environmental History Review,*16 (1992): 28–52.

Wright, Angus. *The Death of Ramón González: The Modern Agricultural Dilemma.* 2nd ed. Austin: University of Texas Press, 2005.

Direct Marketing by Small Farmers in Central and Southern Mexico

Food First/Institute for Food and Development Policy. *Organic Vegetables for Export to Texas Summary of Business Plan.* Unpublished document.

___. *Pilot Project to Establish a Mexico-U.S. market for Sustainable Foods.* Unpublished document.

___. *Project Feasibility Study: Agro-ecological Production for Export, San Luis Coyotzingo Puebla, Mexico, English Summary.* Unpublished document. February 2008.

Holt-Giménez, Eric. Meeting at Food First/Institute for Food and Development Policy, Oakland, CA, June 5, 2008.

Genetically Engineered Corn in Mexico

Altieri, Miguel. *Genetic Engineering in Agriculture: The Myths, Environmental Risks, and Alternatives.* 2nd ed. Oakland, CA: Food First Books, 2004.

Carlsen, Laura. "The Movement to Defend Traditional Maize." Interhemispheric Resource Center Americas Program. *The Americas This Week,* June 24, 2004. http://americas.irc-online.org/columns/amprog/2004/0406maize.html.

The Global Center The Center for Grassroots Oversight. "Profile: Ministry of the Environment and Natural Resources." *History Commons.* 2008. http://complete911timeline.org/entity.jsp?entity=ministry_of_the_environment_and_natural_resources.

Federal Ministry of Education and Research. "Mexico: Outcrossing of Genetically Modified Maize." *GMO Safety: Genetic engineering—Plants—Environment.* February 10, 2003. http://www.gmo-safety.eu/en/maize/outcrossing/101.docu.html.

Fox, Maggie. "No GM Crops Where Corn Was Born." *Independence* [South Africa], August 9, 2005. http://www.int.iol.co.za/index.php?set_id=14&click_id=143&art_id=qw1123577102693B251.

Hansen, Michael, K. *Genetic Engineering Is Not an Extension of Conventional Plant Breeding: How Genetic Engineering Differs from Conventional Breeding, Hybridization, Wide Crosses and Horizontal Gene Transfer.* Consumer Policy

Institute/Consumers Union, January 2000. http://www.gene.ch/info4action/2000/Feb/msg00028.html.

The International Foundation for the Conservation of Natural Resources. "Greenpeace and Biotech: Truth or Deliberate Scare," IFCNR Biotech website, June 2, 2002. http://biotech.ifcnr.com/article.cfm?NewsID=279.

Kaiser, Jocelyn. "Mexican Corn Invasion Vanishes." *ScienceNOW* (2005): 1. http://sciencenow.sciencemag.org/cgi/content/full/2005/808/1.

Kinchy, Abby. "Making Transgenes Visible: Knowledge Work in the Movement against Genetically Modified Corn in Mexico." A paper presented at the American Sociological Association Conference, Montreal Convention Center, Montreal, Quebec, Canada, August 11, 2006. http://www.allacademic.com/meta/p105360_index.html.

Marrero, Carmelo Ruiz. Interhemispheric Resource Center Americas Program. *Biodiversity in Danger: The Genetic Contamination of Mexican Maize.* June 11, 2004. Center for International Policy. http://americas.irc-online.org/am/1636.

Marris, Emma. "Four Years On, No Transgenes Found in Mexican Maize." *Nature*, August 8, 2005.

Massarani, Luisa. "No Evidence GM Genes Are Still in Local Mexican Maize." *SciDev.Net*, August 9, 2005. http://www.scidev.net/en/news/no-evidence-gm-genes-are-still-in-local-mexican.html.

Prakash, C.S. "Duh . . . No GM Genes in Mexican Corn." *AgBioView*, August 9, 2005. http://www.agbioworld.org/newsletter_wm/index.php?caseid=archive&newsid=2398.

Quist, D., and Ignacio H. Chapela. "Transgenic DNA Introgressed into Traditional Maize Landraces in Oaxaca, Mexico." *Nature* 414 (2001): 541–43.

"Genetically Modified Maize Not Found in Southern Mexico." *ScienceDaily*, August 12, 2005. http://www.sciencedaily.com/releases/2005/08/050811105417.htm.

Wirz, Johannes. "The Case of Mexican Maize." The Nature Institute. *In Context* 9 (2003): 3–5. http://www.natureinstitute.org/pub/ic/ic9/maize.htm.

Yoon, Carol Kaesuk. "Genetic Modification Taints Corn in Mexico." *New York Times*, October 2, 2001. http://www.biotech-info.net/mexico_corn.html.

Zaid, A., et al. *Glossary of Biotechnology and Genetic Engineering.* FAO Research and Technology Paper No. 7. Rome: Food and Agriculture Organization of the United Nations, 1999.

About the Author

Dori Stone is a graduate of the University of California at Davis where she studied International Agricultural Development. Dori participated in a reality tour from El Paso to Oaxaca led by Food First executive director, Eric Holt-Giménez in the summer of 2007. The purpose of the tour was to gain a better understanding of the factors driving so many despairing farmers to abandon their homes and families to come to the U.S. to work, and to explore the impact of their absence on those who remain in Mexico. Dori's book, *Beyond the Fence: A Journey to the Roots of the Migration Crisis* documents that trip, and like many good travelogues, raises questions and ponders possibilities.

About Food First

Food First, also known as the Institute for Food and Development Policy, is a nonprofit research and education-for-action center dedicated to investigating and exposing the root causes of hunger in a world of plenty. It was founded in 1975 by Frances Moore Lappé, author of the bestseller Diet for a Small Planet, and food policy analyst, Dr. Joseph Collins. Food First research has revealed that hunger is created by concentrated economic and political power, not by scarcity. Resources and decision making are in the hands of a wealthy few, depriving the majority of land and jobs, and therefore of food.

Hailed by The New York Times as "one of the most established food think tanks in the country," Food First has grown to profoundly shape the debate about hunger and development.

But Food First is more than a think tank. Through books, reports, videos, media, and public speaking, Food First experts not only reveal the often hidden roots of hunger, they show how individuals can get involved in bringing an end to hunger. Food First inspires action by bringing to light the efforts of people and their organizations around the world who are creating farming and food systems that truly meet people's needs.

More Books From Food First

Alternatives to the Peace Corps: A Guide to Global Volunteer
Opportunities, Twelfth Edition
Edited by Caitlin Hachmyer
Newly expaned and updated, this easy-to-use guidebook is the origi-
nal resource for finding community-based, grassroots volunteer
work—the kind of work that changes the world, one person at a time.
Paperback, $11.95

Campesino a Campesino: Voices from Latin America's Farmer to Farmer
Movement for Sustainable Agriculture
Eric Holt-Giménez
The voices and stories of dozens of farmers are captured in this first
written history of the farmer-to-farmer movement, which describes
the social, political, economic, and environmental
circumstances that shape it.
Paperback, $19.95

Promised Land: Competing Visions of Agrarian Reform
Edited by Peter Rosset, Raj Patel, and Michael Courville
Agrarian reform is back at the center of the national and rural devel-
opment debate. The essays in this volume critically analyze
a wide range of competing visions of land reform.
Paperback, $21.95

Sustainable Agriculture and Resistance: Transforming Food Production
in Cuba
**Edited by Fernando Funes, Luis García, Martin Bourque, Nilda Pérez, and
Peter Rosset**
Unable to import food or farm chemicals and machines in the wake
of the Soviet bloc's collapse and a tightening US embargo, Cuba
turned toward sustainable agriculture, organic farming, urban gardens, and other techniques to secure its food supply. This book gives
details of that remarkable achievement.
Paperback, $18.95

The Future in the Balance: Essays on Globalization and Resistance
Walden Bello. Edited with a preface by Anuradha Mittal
> A collection of essays by global south activist and scholar Walden Bello on the myths of development as prescribed by the World Trade Organization and other institutions, and the possibility of another world based on fairness and justice.
> Paperback, $13.95

Views from the South: The Effects of Globalization and the WTO on Third World Countries
Edited by Sarah Anderson
Foreword by Jerry Mander. Afterword by Anuradha Mittal
> This rare collection of essays by activists and scholars from the global south describes, in pointed detail, the effects of the WTO and other Bretton Woods institutions.
> Paperback, $12.95

Basta! Land and the Zapatista Rebellion in Chiapas, Third Edition
George A. Collier with Elizabeth Lowery-Quaratiello
Foreword by Peter Rosset
> The classic on the Zapatistas in its third edition, including a preface by Rodolfo Stavenhagen.
> Paperback, $16.95

America Needs Human Rights
Edited by Anuradha Mittal and Peter Rosset
> This anthology includes writings on understanding human rights, poverty and welfare reform in America.
> Paperback, $13.95

The Paradox of Plenty: Hunger in a Bountiful World
Edited by Douglas H. Boucher
> Excerpts from Food First's best writings on world hunger and what we can do to change it.
> Paperback, $18.95

Education for Action: Undergraduate and Graduate Programs that Focus on Social Change, Fourth Edition
Edited by Joan Powell
> An updated authoritative and easy-to-use guidebook that provides information on progressive programs in a wide variety of fields.
> Paperback, $12.95

We encourage you to buy Food First Books from your local independent bookseller; if they don't have them in stock, they can usually order them for you fast. To find an independent bookseller in your area, go to www.booksense.com.

Food First books are also available through major online booksellers (Powell's, Amazon, and Barnes and Noble), and through the Food First website, www.foodfirst.org. You can also order direct from our distributor, Perseus Distribution, at (800) 343-4499. If you have trouble locating a Food First title, write, call, or e-mail us:

Food First
398 60th Street
Oakland, CA 94618-1212 USA
Tel: (510) 654-4400
Fax: (510) 654-4551
E-mail: foodfirst@foodfirst.org
Web: www.foodfirst.org

If you are a bookseller or other reseller, contact our distributor, Perseus Distribution, at (800) 343-4499, to order.

Films from Food First

The Greening of Cuba
Jaime Kibben
A profiling of Cuban farmers and scientists working to reinvent a sustainable agriculture based on ecological principles and local knowledge.
DVD (In Spanish with English subtitles), $35.00

America Needs Human Rights
A film told in the voices of welfare mothers, homeless men and women, low-wage workers, seniors, veterans, and health care workers.
DVD, $19.95

Caminos: The Immigrant's Trail
Juan Carlos Zaldivar
Stories of Mexican farmers who were driven off their land, forced to leave their families and risk their lives to seek work in the U.S.
DVD and Study Guide, $20.00

How to Become a Member
or Intern of Food First

Join Food First

Private contributions and membership gifts fund the core of Food First/Institute for Food and Development Policy's work. Each member strengthens Food First's efforts to change a hungry world. We invite you to join Food First. As a member you will receive a 20 percent discount on all Food First books. You will also receive our quarterly publications, Food First News and Views and Backgrounders, providing information for action on current food and hunger crises in the United States and around the world. If you want to subscribe to our Internet newsletter, People Putting Food First, send us an e-mail at foodfirst@foodfirst.org. All contributions are tax deductible.

You are also invited to give a gift membership to others interested in the fight to end hunger. **www.foodfirst.org**

Become an Intern for Food First

There are opportunities for interns in research, advocacy, campaigning, publishing, computers, media, and publicity at Food First. Our interns come from around the world. They are a vital part of the organization and make the work possible.

To become a member or apply to become an intern, just call, visit our website, or clip and return the attached coupon to:

Food First
398 60th Street
Oakland, CA 94618-1212 USA
Tel: (510) 654-4400
Web: www.foodfirst.org